UNBROKEN

Navigating the Madness of Family Dysfunction, Addiction, Alcoholism, and Heartache

Annie Highwater

FREEDOM FOX PRESS
Dancing Lemur Press, L.L.C.
Pikeville, North Carolina
www.dancinglemurpress.com

Dedication

To Scottie and Jeff, who fill the biggest spaces of my heart

In loving memory of Wally and Butch, unexpected friends who became family. Both came along right on time and left their mark forever

And to anyone facing a crisis of family who needs the reminder to keep getting up and pressing on. Families do recover.

Table of Contents

Acknowledgments

My life was renovated and rebuilt by truth and kindness. For that I want to extend my deep gratitude to those who were part of the building process.

Most High, Loving Kindness, Creator, Father, Shepherd, Protector, Counselor, Comforter, Friend... Source of my strength, peace, recovery, health and courage; in You, *because* of You I live and breathe and have my being. You have created dignity, credibility, worth, and confidence where once there was none.

Scottie, my family jewel, your life gives me so much joy. You are living proof that success and strength are worth the struggle. Thank you for your presence on this earth! No one holds as much space in my mind, heart or soul as you. You have an effect on those around you like the sun bursting through after a long, dark storm. I wouldn't change one thing about you; I love you so very much! May love, sunshine and happiness always surround you when you're far from home. Don't ever give up!

Dad, my corner coach, your strength and rugged determination stick with me still. You were all heart. Until we meet again—I hope I make you proud.

Mom, may the rest of your days be the best of your days! To the degree my life is blessed, I hope to enrich yours far beyond it!

Jeff, I could not get by in this world without you! You have stood beside me through so much. Sometimes silently, often at a loss for what to say or how to handle my anguish, but nonetheless you stuck by me like no one ever has. Always at my finish lines, always cheering me on and making me laugh through some of the hardest days and most embarrassing moments. You help me see life through a better lens. Always reminding me to relax, not to think too deeply about what anyone thinks, and to realize that *no one* has it all together, all the time. I will spend the rest of my life thankful for you!

Keelie, my constant companion of love, friendship, comfort and loyalty. Twelve years you walked beside me. You were a loss felt as deep as any person. There is no such thing as "just a dog" for those of us loved by one. Many days you were all I came home to. Your sweet, little life taught me everything about unconditional love and the quiet presence of comfort. Your death taught me about letting go. There will never be another like you.

Dr. Dominique, you are intelligence, strength, and compassion absolutely *personified*. I am deeply grateful to have met someone like you! I don't know what I would do without you, the Allies in Recovery team, CRAFT, and all you have taught me.

Pam, your counsel speaks volumes to me still. How would I ever have untangled if not for you? Thank you for the wisdom you spoke into my life—your words have never left me! You changed my life forever.

Kell, brother, friend, neighbor, Pit bull! Your "Take no SH*T" personality is my constant reminder not to take any myself!

Shell, sister and friend who showed up many times or listened to me yell through the phone all I felt was going wrong! Thank you for believing with me that the tide would turn. It did! It still is.

My other siblings, thank you for being the iron that sharpens me to strive for the best life possible.

Lori, the first person I ever told what I had been through. The first person to ever validate it. I don't know if you are even aware of that. I remember our very first conversation and every one of them after. You are such a gentle, soothing soul. I have no doubt that your work in the field of trauma and grief is changing lives forever, you certainly made a lasting impact in mine. I am *beyond* grateful for you!

Wally, you were such a comfort, you made me laugh through the times I felt so hopeless and lost. Your friendship was a gift! I cherish every memory. I can't wait to see you again, I have so much to tell you.

Kathy, I wish we'd have met years before. Thank you for being a comfort, a friend, and as loyal as it gets. Thank you for the cards, calls, texts, and compassion *through it all*. I consider you the sweetest gift from my friend, Wally.

Vince, even though I still sometimes introduce you as "My brother's friend," you are truly more mine! You have consistently been one of the greatest sources of friendship, information, encouragement, and hope since I was just a kid. I am so very thankful for you, for Natalie, and for every moment you've been a part of my story.

Butch and Judy, you could not have known how *needed* your kindness was when our paths first crossed. You taught me that unconditional kindness, comfort, and the protection of neighbors can restore one's confidence. My life drastically improved when I met you.

Jim, you always get me. And even when you don't, out of loyalty you pretend to! Our friendship transcends

9

time, gender, and geography. I am so very grateful for you!

Scott, thank you for all the times you took my calls, responded to my texts, and let me put a voice to the craziness I was feeling when it came to family situations. Could not have asked for a better Ex!

Greg Hannley and SOBA Recovery Centers, how do I thank you for saving us over and over? Your work saving lives—no matter how many times or how long it takes—is **unparalleled**. You are a community of difference makers and life-changers. May your work be rewarded a million times over!

Sandra, what friendship, safety, ease, and comfort you represent. You are a once in a lifetime, rare find.

Michelle M, thank you for making me laugh so hard over the miles we've walked that I sprained my back. You are a one of a kind, hilarious, comedic therapy!

Doug, Joe, and my Wednesday night support family. You have been my lighthouse, my safety zone, my comfort and many times the slap in the face, wake-up call I needed to make progress. You have my loyalty forever.

Barb, my difference making, life-changing third grade teacher. How can I thank someone who taught me to write when I felt overwhelmed, chaotic, upset, and groundless? That should be a class for every child! You made a supernatural difference in my life when you set me on a path to pursue my passion, my purpose, and taught me where to direct my focus when the going gets tough. May life reward you to the millionth power for the difference you have made in mine!

Brenda, the work you do for families, against stigma and on behalf of those we dearly love who suffer with a substance issue, is honorable beyond words! Thank you for putting in the work so that the rest of us feel safe enough to raise a voice.

Laurie, my later in life friend, and recovery partner. I can't imagine life without you, you have taught me so much!

Isabel, oh my goodness your help on this project is worth more than I can ever repay. I cannot thank you enough for your kindness. Your eye for detail amazes me! You are a very special gem.

Monica, a mom like me, on a mission to get the word out to other moms that their son or daughter can make it out of the depths! Thank you for your tenacity and effervescent energy for the cause of spreading hope and information to families desperately needing to recover.

Naomi and all those in my Sunday night support family, I have learned so much from listening every week. We have been on this rollercoaster together and I wouldn't change that for anything. Without every one of your voices I could not have carried on with so much hope!

Julie, what a sweet-spirited, thoughtful friend you have been, placed in my life right on time. You inspire me to be considerate and kind always.

Sandy, listening to your real, raw truths every week encouraged me to aggressively continue to self-examine, rise, and recover. This world could use 100 million more like you!

Lesley and the Freedom Fox publishing team, I can't thank you enough for the work you have done. You have been encouraging, supportive, patient, and enthusiastic while bringing my vision and life's work to the page.

Sherry Gaba as well as the folks at This Life Podcast, Dr. Drew, and Bob Forrest; for educating me every week on how to manage life in the presence of trauma, adversity, and family addiction. Each of you have been a light for the journey.

Super Soul Sunday voices, Brené, Iyanla, India, Beth Moore, and Cheryl Strayed for your telling and writing. You've changed my *soul* forever.

And to all who raise a voice in the fight against the epidemic of addiction devouring families across the nation, for *each* of you I am more than grateful. Courageously you stand as one in the face of fear, stigma, and heartache. In the presence of judgment, you demand answers and action. You declare outrage, truth, and hope. I am proud to stand with you. It takes every voice to make progress, so keep right on telling, talking, speaking, fighting. Keep standing. Families *can* heal. Don't ever give up.

Together we recover!

Foreword

Annie Highwater has made a significant contribution to the growing literature by family members describing life with a loved one addicted to drugs or alcohol. When I finished reading *Unhooked*, I quickly reached out to her, so thrilled was I to read a monograph that had broken new ground.

I told Annie how moved I was by her honest and insightful account of her own painful journey, as her son spiraled out of control with opioids. She describes her early efforts—often herculean—to protect and police her son, all the while trying so carefully to pretend that life was normal...whereas her reality was actually punctuated by gut-crushing crises as her son barreled out of control with illegal and life-threatening drugs. Annie sets the stage by providing the reader a backdrop of her own upbringing and its craziness; to this she adds her own perfect storm of sorts, formed of her own fragile sensitivity and the dance she had embraced: so tight, so entrenched with her son, that it nearly did her in.

As we read about her son's journey, Annie gives us much more than a chronicle of what happened to him, to them. We become privileged observers of a mom on the darkest journey possible: the fight to save her son, the confusion over the advice of others, and the drive for her own survival. *Unhooked* is a memoir speaking to the power and limits of love when faced with another's addiction. *Unhooked* is a memoir of recovery, not just of her son's but of Annie's as well.

It is with great pleasure that I write this forward to Annie's new book. In it, Annie assembles what she learned during this critical period. In a series of brief, poignant essays, Annie lays out the essential tenets you will need when you love someone struggling with addiction.

Annie's passion on this subject is unparalleled. There has never been a more honest and dedicated heroine than Annie. To look within and to emerge victorious, strong and clear: this is what Annie has done for us. These essays are gentle yet powerful insights on how to live with the addiction of another.

The addiction of a loved one intertwines with our own personality, our upbringing and vulnerabilities—it can be crippling. Faced with the gale force of addiction, Annie was determined to find a way to survive, even to thrive.

And survive, and thrive, you must, too. Families caught up in addiction suffer disproportionately from stress-related medical conditions, sleep disturbances, depression and anxiety.

A 2010 study of Kaiser Permanente patients found a strong link between a loved one's addiction and family members' chronic medical and psychiatric ill-health... to the point that more severe addiction correlated with more severe health problems in family members. It's critical that you pay attention to your own health as well. The study showed that with cessation of the addiction, the mental and physical health of the family improved as well. Assessment at five years showed a family doing well and out of the health "high risk" group.

This makes intuitive sense to most of us but it helps to have it quantified and recognized nevertheless.

The world has not paid much attention to the families of those struggling with substance use disorder. And when it does, it has not been very kind. We are pitied and secretly ogled to see what we've done wrong, how we might have contributed to the disorder. We are victims or enablers. The treatment system has marginalized us. We cannot call and make a referral on behalf of a loved one. We are told our loved one has to make the call, for it shows a readiness to enter treatment. Contact with our loved one while in treatment will likely be limited for we may just be bad news. We may need to ask several times for releases to be signed so that we can contribute our ideas, our expert opinion really, and even then we may be dismissed. And in the end, we will likely be called on to be the untrained transitional care person for them, as the fragmented system of care creates silos and there is suddenly nowhere for our loved one to go.

Yet I also believe we—the families—are the secret resource this country is failing to grasp. We are perhaps 200 million strong and we have the potential to influence our loved one towards treatment and recovery. That's what Annie and I collaborate on today: we teach families how to create an environment around their addicted loved one—an environment that is the most conducive to recovery. It is called CRAFT and we teach it online at AlliesinRecovery.net.

CRAFT uses a scientifically validated approach made up of behaviorism—how you communicate and respond to your Loved One—and the principles that lead to a successful, no-cost treatment intervention. But for all this to work, you will need to be strong, calm, and centered. You'll need to save your energy for what works and have both feet in hope. You will need to feel better now, not just once your loved one gets to recovery. And for this to happen, Annie has given us this book. She has given us the road map for how best to care for a loved one struggling with addiction: the secret is in caring first for ourselves.

Written by Dominique Simon-Levine, a Ph.D. substance abuse researcher, who is in long-term recovery. She runs an award-winning program for families called Allies in Recovery. Founded in 2003, Allies in Recovery has helped hundreds of families to climb out of the abyss of addiction. Her work is featured on HBO and on www.alliesinrecovery.net

Introduction

Many of us know the sorrow of family dysfunction. Rejection, jealousy, abandonment, deception, accusation, betrayal, meanness...even *hatred* from those who are expected to love us. When wounds come from the ones we're supposed to feel safe with, it's a pain that cuts deep and runs long. Whether stemming from the turmoil of divorce, a misunderstanding, conflict, a strained relationship with a parent, sibling, or child, or when volatile issues are related to mental illness and addiction; the issues of family stress hang over us like a heavy, dark cloud.

There's no spike of adrenaline quite like going from zero to sixty with a family member. I'm certainly no stranger to it. In fact, when it comes to dysfunction, specifically regarding a family member with an addiction, I know the journey by heart. I know the path like a road from back home. I was born on it. I have run, walked, crawled and balled myself up in a heap of defeat upon it. It's a road I've traveled all my life. Having spent holidays alone in a puddle of tears, and many years with family relationships so fractured we didn't know one another's phone number, I indeed know the heartache. It's etched into who I am.

Due to dysfunction, mental and emotional illness and the destruction caused by addiction, I have spent most of my adult life on the outside of family. A virtual stranger to those I grew up with in the same house. Addiction has deprived me of a healthy relationship with my mother and sent my only son 3,000 miles across the country to find his way to health and recovery (following a sports injury that resulted in a nightmare opiate dependency). When it comes to having a heart broken over family, I *know* the road of sorrow and despair.

Nevertheless...

I believe the road can turn. I believe in breakthrough and progress. I believe in healing and recovery. But more than anything I believe in *hope*. Hope in the midst of despair. I can say that in the worst midnight hours, even still there was hope. Hope was the small flame within that refused to burn out. Hope. It's what I fastened myself to when it seemed like everyone around me was losing their mind and my spirit was breaking alongside them.

There are times in our lives when we will need to prop ourselves up on hope, comforting ourselves with the faith that things won't always be traumatic and terrible. I discovered what strength this hope has in the middle of a barren time of isolation, despair, and family estrangement. I learned that the seed of hope stands stronger and fights harder than just about any force coming against it.

Unbroken chronicles my journey from drowning in heartache, to latching onto hope, to rising in triumph and restoration. I have poured out what I learned in the misery of the midnight hour, along with hope, strength, and health gleaned from therapy and recovery support rooms.

The healing process was not linear, but it was exact and permanent. Similarly, Unbroken can be read out of order by chapter topic, or chronologically from beginning to end, whatever your heart feels drawn to. May you find *your* seed of hope within these pages, and the encouragement to hold on for one more day, one more hour, to try one more time. To fight to believe long enough to see your breakthrough, no matter how miserable and dark the days might seem.

And after the storms, may you find your spirit not only unbroken, but **unbreakable**.

Chapter 1

I Feel Like I'm Drowning. Will I Live Through This?

This is a question no one can answer for you. In fact, I think it's a question that no one wants us asking. We watch eyes glaze over and people become uncomfortably uninterested when we give our rundown of the darkest areas of life.

When one particularly dark season began in my life, I found myself first asking only the inky black ceiling above my bed at night, "I'm sinking, I feel like I'm drowning...will I *live* through this?" Silence. Warm tears made their way down my temples into my hair as night after night I wondered where I'd find hope.

In less than a year I found my life gutted, along with my heart, my hope, and my life's plans. Despair, hopelessness, and fear hung over every moment of every day.

Crisis and grief for me seem like drowning. In those times I feel as if I couldn't find my footing. Life felt groundless, bottomless, overwhelming as I fought to stabilize, to breathe, all the while sinking.

I remember these feelings of terror as a child a time or two in the neighborhood swimming pool. Finding myself in water too deep and knowing I was in trouble. Once I realized I was in well over my head, panic would hit. I never forgot the feeling of being totally out of control; it was a feeling of terror, of *primal* fear.

I seemed to struggle with the panic almost as much as I fought to make my way up and out of the deep water. Once I found solid footing (or a more skilled swimmer would grab my arm and pull me to safety), relief would wash over me like a warm bath. I was suddenly thankful and aware of every breath I could take.

In my most overwhelming season of life, those around me would ask, "How are you...*really?*" I found myself saying "I feel like I'm drowning."

It can be interesting to research and study metaphors in life and nature that may relate to our circumstances. Sometimes that will lead to clues of how to cope. I researched "What happens when you drown." And discovered several survivor stories from people who had almost died from drowning. To my amazement, all of the experiences I found held something in common. The survivor described that as soon as they stopped resisting, almost the very second that they ceased violently thrashing and flailing about or trying to grab a hold of *anything* they could find for support and safety in their desperate struggle to survive, a calming peace overcame them.

It was described as a peace like no other. Peace that surpasses understanding, and would seem improbable as one is fighting for their life.

I found a message in a bottle within this description. When we continue struggling and fighting circumstances that we have done all we *possibly can* to change or improve, we sink further into them. When continuing to resist and struggle we remain stuck in misery and madness. Notably anything (and at times, *anyone*) we grip onto for rescue is often a slippery disappointment.

Sometimes those who appear to be a life raft turns

out to be an anvil, pulling us further down.

Resisting circumstances that we are powerless to change perpetuates our most acidic of emotions. Especially when we are drowning in the *deep*, horrendous waters of grief and pain that may involve loss, betrayal, or fear. These waters for me often include worries about my adult son living across the country from us, or maybe the desperation to resolve a miserable conflict that might be consuming my thoughts.

Sometimes it's a financial burden that jolts us awake in the middle of the night with panic and dread, or possibly a health issue that brings life as we knew it to a screeching halt. It can be a relationship or family issue that is in miserable condition resulting in repeated heartache and anxiety. I've experienced them all (sometimes all at once). These are deep, dark, *icy* waters to navigate.

"Will I live through this?" I found myself asking those closest to me. "Will it get better? When? *When* will it get better?" The various "I don't know" answers feel like weights added to our struggle for air.

Life has seasons and seasons change. The sooner we stop thrashing about within the season we're in, the sooner we will find the calm. When we have done all we know to do, when we stop fighting and resisting the things *we cannot change* and instead accept life on life's terms—*as it is*—the sooner we are able to allow ourselves to float along with the current and find our way forward.

Acceptance. I find that's when peace comes. We can take a full breath once we stop fighting. That is when stable footing appears. And sometimes even rescue.

"Accepting the things we cannot change will bring us

the peace we long for." ~ Unknown

God, grant me the serenity to accept the things I cannot change,

Courage to change the things I can,

And wisdom to know the difference.

Chapter 2
Needing Support

How important is support? I believe nature reveals to us that we are *meant* to support one another along the journey of life. Dolphins, for instance, are known to work together to catch fish, save sick friends, and play. Recently researchers have recorded the clever cetaceans 'talking' to each other in order to solve a complex puzzle. The discovery suggests dolphins use a language dedicated to problem solving. I read an observation report about one dolphin becoming paralyzed, when others saw that it was unable to swim, they gathered to form a bridge of support under it, carefully raising their injured friend to the surface for air.

Joshua Plotnik, a behavioral ecologist at Mahidol University in Thailand, and primatologist Frans de Waal, director of Emory University's Living Links Center, have shown through a controlled study what those who work with elephants have always believed: the animals offer something akin to human sympathetic concern when observing distress in another, including their relatives and friends. Elephants in another herd were once found solemnly gathered in a circle, weeping together over the body of one of their herd who had died.

Along with dolphins and elephants, gorillas, dogs, cats, certain corvids (the bird group that includes ravens), and squirrels among others, have been shown to recognize when a herd mate is upset, weakened, or injured and to offer gentle caresses and chirps of sympathy, according to a study (published February 18 in the online journal *PeerJ*).

In nature, lending comfort and support seems to come, well...natural.

Some years back I personally observed comfort and support from nonhumans when my beloved Cairn terrier injured her spine, became paralyzed, and went through major corrective surgery. She recovered, yet never regained full strength. For the next four years of her life I tended to her every need as my other dog and our cat watched over her closely. They stuck by her, ever present at her side, especially when she grew weaker or sick. I often found them sleeping one on each side of her, laying close against her.

When she later died, for months the two of them would sit with me in every room I occupied, something they hadn't done together before. Every day they would lay at my feet, one on either side, as I worked my way through the sadness and misery of losing my closest companion. That little dog had been like a baby to me. Because of her many health issues I took care of her like a child. In some ways, caring for her had even become a distracting comfort when my son moved across the country. Losing her was a traumatic shock. I was touched by how aware the remaining two were of my grief. Their loyal presence helped me get through that difficult time. Animals somehow sense when we are in need of extra comfort.

Another example I read not long ago was in reference to Redwood trees having surprisingly shallow roots compared to other trees. Redwood trees are some of the tallest, strongest trees, yet they have short roots that grow more wide than deep. However, these roots have an amazing ability to latch onto one another, growing tightly together as a strong force underground. The linking of roots allows for added strength, causing several trees to unite as a whole, standing together as one when storms come.

I. Love. That.

Nature gets it. So if support and comfort are vital in *nature;* what message does that send to us?

What a beautiful thing if that kind of support came naturally in *every* family and group setting. How much different would our lives be if we instinctively came together to raise each other up, without considering fault, blame, or shame, without thinking of our personal issues or awkward feelings. How wonderful would it be if we didn't hold back, but instead showed up, putting opinions and differences aside to offer comfort and encouragement, rallying around someone in need. How much stronger we would be when the storms come.

I've most often found unconditional support in rooms of recovery. Managing the adversities of life feels crushing, especially when you feel like you have to do it by yourself. Having reliable group support can provide great comfort in challenging times.

For most of my life I'd taught myself to have a stiff upper lip and push through trials. Therefore, support was most often reserved for a small handful of friends, Google, or the self-help section of the Library. It was by chance that I started attending family recovery meetings. We had already come through so much of the storm by the time I started going. But once I went, I never left. Supportive meetings were the final puzzle piece in my walk forward out of years of misery and dysfunction. They were a perfect fit.

After experiencing the profoundly healing effects of attending a good, solid support group, I now admit I regret the nights I walked the floors alone, agonizing about our circumstances (as detailed in my book "Unhooked"). I regret not having a safe place to vent my frustration or hear how others coped when dealing with their own. How I wish I had a room to go to from the beginning of the journey, to gather with people going through what I was going through. I would have found safety in those numbers and strength from others who could say "Yep, I've been there. That happened to me too. You're not the only one. I get it."

I did have very good friends to call and I was lucky enough to personally know a few professionals I could contact in a pinch. Yet, had I also been rooted around those going through the same dark waters I was drowning in, I believe it would have made navigating my way through them a lot easier. There's just something about someone who has walked the same road telling you *"It will be okay"* that is truly worth its weight in gold.

We are some years past the havoc of addiction first raging through our home. But I still regularly meet with a group for support. Now that life is more calm and stable, I believe listening as well as giving comfort, encouragement, and hope back is a great way to keep a stream of kindness flowing. No one should have to go through the harsh times of life alone. That's when we need others to build a bridge under us and raise us up, especially when we're feeling paralyzed. There are also times we're called to be part of that bridge and help lift someone else up. Support is give and take. We all need it; we all need to offer it.

It's not weak to admit you need some support, actually it's strong. It's real. And that's not always easy; it takes courage. Being real is not for the phony or faint of heart.

The epidemic of addiction our nation is experiencing is not stopping or even slowing down. I believe it's awakening us to our need to be open, honest, and to compassionately support one another. Thankfully support groups are becoming more available. I strongly encourage everyone to research and find one that is a fit for you. Online or in person. We need all the strength available! Life can be brutal; it helps when you're not alone. Support can make all the difference.

We need people to understand and care. That is where healing happens and strength develops. It's as simple as that.

"Friendship is born at the moment when one person says to another, 'What! You too? I thought I was the only one.'" ~ *C.S. Lewis*

Let's root for one another.

Chapter 3

Drama, Drama, Drama: You Define Drama!

Yes, that is right, *you* define it. Drama means something different to us all. I discovered the deeply personal meaning drama can have while researching the subject. I spent a week asking random people who crossed my path, **"What is your definition of 'drama'?"**

Responses were profound. Some were passionate and intense, some were comical. Many times the question prompted personal examples of injustice, pain, and conflict. All answers were heartfelt and genuine. (I've included some of the answers in and after this section.)

This is a highly personalized question—people seemed to most often define drama by what bothers them.

Unless you were born and raised alone in the woods with no human interaction, you have at some point in your life experienced *drama*.

Webster's dictionary defines "drama" as:

1 In literature- the portrayal of life or character, to tell a story usually involving conflicts and emotions, typically designed for theatrical performance. 2 A movie or television performance. 3 A state, situation or series of events involving interesting or intense conflict of forces, i.e. details of "the drama of the past week" or "one is dealing with some family drama" – "Drama" Merriam-Webster.com. 2011. https://www.merriam-webster.com

(31 January 2018).

M, a corporate computer programmer, defined drama as *"An unnecessary emotional response to a situation. A response that stimulates negative or unwanted excitement and emotions in others"*

Conflict and intense emotions are commonly associated with drama.

B, a family addiction recovery expert, said *"Drama is an emotional reaction far in excess of what is truly warranted"*

We all know there are various types of drama, some of the most extreme occurs in relation to an addicted loved one. This type presents chaos, conflict, and crisis and can induce sadness, shame, anger, and terror like nothing else. Support and education for those who have a loved one struggling with addiction and SUD is critical.

But there can be excess drama in all types of human relationships; drama in the home, on the job, in social settings. Like a lot of people, I experienced drama during a childhood filled with crisis and dysfunction.

"Any situation that causes my stress and anxiety level to escalate unnecessarily!" ~ S, Firefighter

Conflict and charged emotions are an occasional part of the experience of life. But *crisis*-level chaos, as well as *unnecessary* negativity and dysfunction, do not have to be the norm. Recovery and therapy help us heal, cope, and develop positive ways of managing situations once packed with drama in order to live a more peaceful existence.

It's important to realize that it's absolutely possible to avoid recurring conflict and drama in our lives.

"People making a big deal out of nothing" ~ C, designer

There are people who seem to be attracted to drama. Almost as if they enjoy it and can't seem to live without it. They will always have it. The types who don't seem to be motivated for peace but instead get energy from chaos. People who start drama regularly, stir it up, join in when it's not their business, and keep the issues going, stoking the fires of strife.

These are not the peacemakers of life. They're the types you can enjoy knowing and absolutely care about, but it's not wise to remain close if you are in pursuit of a calm life.

"Someone who naturally overreacts to very little stimulus." ~ L, CEO

When I found my own life in no short supply of drama, I began looking inward to figure out what I had the ability to control, change, or resolve. I knew things had to change and felt that the changes had to start with me. Dysfunctional behaviors, reactions, thought processes, and some unhealthy people I mistakenly thought cared about me, had to go.

This is an as needed, custom fit process.

When drama occurs in our lives, we need to ask: *What am I attracting? What am I tolerating? And why?* Along with, *What am I contributing to the problems?* Pondering the answers sheds light on areas we can take action to improve.

A major solution can be to **avoid interacting closely with negativity; only acknowledge and engage with positives.**

This does not diminish the need to have boundaries, consequences, or protect and defend yourself when necessary. Nor does it mean passively allowing anyone to use or abuse you. This simply means: **Refusing to interact or engage with negative, nasty drama.**

Don't take the bait, don't take the hooks, don't give dysfunction in return for dysfunction.

Negative drama will keep going even if you have a spreadsheet filled with proof that you are right. You won't win. Drama begets more drama. Positive reinforcement paired with healthy boundaries and a wall up against negative behavior will promote peace.

This is not always easy, particularly if we come from a hostile environment. Becoming an expert at *not* interacting with negativity doesn't happen overnight.

To be very real about it, there are still times when I'm strongly triggered or feeling tired and weak, I can be susceptible to pettiness and drama. But the baseline intent is to be wiser and healthier. We can drop the ball now and then; that's just part of being human.

When this happens, get up, make amends, and do the next right thing.

"Drama is someone who sees the negative, worst case scenario in every situation, someone who takes all things deeply personal." ~ C, law enforcement

We might have intense emotions and lose our cool to conflict in a moment of weakness, but we don't have to live a *lifestyle* of drama, and we can be mindful to not take everything in life personally.

"People who complain about a situation they created themselves." ~ N, homemaker

There is a difference between someone who can *be* drama, versus someone who *is* drama. Someone who is reacting with intensity is not the same as someone looking to start drama, join it, or prolong it. This is similar to the difference between a person who can get jealous within a situation, versus someone who always seems to be jealous and competitive without appropriate reason.

R, from HR, said *"teenage girls."* (Interesting that boys were not included—they too can be known for drama!)

Children can be taught to be over-reactive with excess drama. If kids are raised around conflict and witness out of control, emotional reactions as a standard, they will often manage future situations in a similar fashion. If, as the adult, our every reaction is emotionally intense and we have a habit of taking things very personally, hitting the ceiling over perceived slights and insults, the children observing us will learn to manage life that way as well. Or they will involve themselves with people who do.

H, medical admin, says *"When I think of drama I think of constant turmoil, of everything **always** being an ordeal."*

Not everything is an ordeal to be registered on the Richter scale! Take a breath before responding, calm down first, or maybe hold an ice cube until it melts in your hands. Simply taking a few moments to pull away and *breathe* before reacting makes all the difference not only within us, but within the situations at hand.

(Note: regardless of the situation or reasons, no one has a right to scream, curse, or name call. If those are your tactics for conflict, you've got it wrong. Period.)

"People freaking out about little things." ~ M, Design

Overreaction, conflict, heated emotional responses, and *unnecessary* problems were repeatedly mentioned when defining drama. These dynamics are guaranteed to disrupt the peace in our lives. These behaviors are also dashboard lights directing us toward what needs to be healed or resolved.

A, corporate office manager, defined drama as *"My bitter sister-in-law."*

Emotional drama not handled in healthy ways leads to bitterness and misery.

It's important to do soul searching and self-work so we don't grow bitter and become so blinded by that bitterness that we unload a poisoned spirit on everyone we encounter. We have all seen that level of misery imbedded in the personality of someone who hasn't dealt with emotional issues or injuries in healthy ways. Recovery and therapy help us maneuver through the drama and release bitterness.

These days, the effects of drama, chaos, and dysfunction are for me now far more benign than they ever were due to the work I've done to increase peace in my life. The same things that used to flatten me or launch me through the ceiling have become much less noticeable, more easily shrugged off. We can get to the point where we recover from the upset a lot quicker. What used to hurt deeply and hurl us into anger and despair for weeks doesn't have to last through the day.

Peace is possible; it's a process. Therapy, research, education, and recovery work are profoundly effective tools for creating a healthy, peaceful life. Recovery and therapy do *work!* Drama doesn't have to call the shots—peace is *possible.*

Other relatable "What is your definition of drama?" answers:

"Arguing with someone in active addiction!" ~ D, Family Counselor

"People being annoying." ~ H, computer technology

"A blown up, exaggerated version of life events!" ~ K, retired

"Unnecessary conflict caused by rumors, hearsay and gossip which results in a lot of wasted time and energy for all parties involved!" ~ C, human resources

"Drama is unneeded frustration." ~ J, carpentry

"People at work who constantly need to be up the boss's butt." ~ D, law enforcement

"When I have to go to the bathroom in a meeting." ~ J, finance and sales

"People bickering back and forth (especially in my presence, especially family bickering...in my presence.)" ~ J, finance

"Drama is the reality show Jersey Shore." ~ S, tech worker

"Emotions." ~ A, VP of communications

"Trouble, I stay away from drama, I get away from anyone associated with it, drama brings nothing but trouble." ~ K, IT director

"Anyone who disrupts a situation for self-acknowledgment." ~ L, HR

"The true definition would be a play, the theater, but we now think of it as craziness, a person who is a hot mess." ~ G, retail designer

"High emotions." ~ S, Communications and media

"The silent treatment." T, U.S. Air Force

"People making a big deal over little things." ~ M, high school student

"A distressing situation someone causes." ~ S, artist

"Office gossip, office cliques and troublemakers at work." L, financial controller

"Lots of anxiety. People who go batsh*t crazy over nothing." ~ D, architecture

"People who bring up politics on social media!" ~ K, restaurant manager

"People who stir the pot and create...drama." ~ M, creative design artist

"When everyone makes <u>their</u> problems mine! Especially money related!" V, teacher

"When an ex talks about their issues and grievances with you in front of your kids." ~ D, real estate

"When someone publicly has a disagreement with another. The disagreement then entangles other people as the parties try and back up their arguments. This drama leads to more drama, leading to uncomfortable situations for all." S, in sales *(Further prodding revealed this was about a family argument on a Facebook post that went off the rails)*

One person sent a screen shot of an extremely personal Facebook status their brother posted and simply said: *"This."*

"Confusion." ~ J, marketing

"Backstabbing." ~ J, pharmaceutical industry

"Overreacting." ~ M, psychologist

A few responses were someone's first name

"I don't have a definition." ~ T, attorney said with an ornery smile. (Not wanting to reveal what bothers him apparently!)

"A play?" ~ C, Sales

My favorite answer:

A young up and coming professional said *"Drama to me would be defined as chaotic energy or in other words...a conversation with my Mom."* That was my son. (I told him I was keeping it, even if he only meant the first part of the definition!)

My definitions: Dysfunction, chaos, conflict, unending upset. Creating trouble where there is none. Extending conflict versus resolving it and finding peace. Disliking or attacking someone without solid reason. Conflict for the sake of conflict. People who constantly cause a disruption of peace.

Chapter 4

Believe It or Not, It's Not Personal

"I *hate* you! You are *the worst* mother ever! You're a terrible *dad!* You're such a #@%$#!! This is ALL *your* fault!"

Sound familiar? This could be your angry son or daughter. Could be a teen, an adult, an addicted loved one. Whoever is spewing, it leaves you feeling like you drank poison and then took a stomach punch from Mike Tyson.

There was a time in my own life when my soul was a sponge for the vicious spewing of vitriol; it was rampant in my family. I was constantly trying to manage or sidestep chaos and conflict. I would absorb it, take it to heart, try everything to resolve it, and spend hours analyzing it. That does not serve one well when dealing with behaviors that addiction can cause. It can take time to untangle from these dynamics and create a life void of craziness. Untangling is a process.

These days I talk with a lot of people going through it and I hear all the same experiences. Details vary, dynamics don't. Certain gut-wrenching things occur when you have dysfunction and/or addiction in your family. Even more if it resides in your home. Things go missing, there is pressure to provide money, and arguments over car keys, rides, who's at fault for what, answers that don't add up, and so on. The presence of addiction completely changes the trajectory of a family and can turn a once peaceful atmosphere upside down and inside out.

Here's an email I received from a worn out mother:

Hi Annie;

So my daughter called this morning. She wanted to use my credit card for work clothes and said she would repay me in a few weeks. I didn't want to do it this time. I know the routine, she will return the clothes for cash and once again I won't ever see a dime of my money. I said no. She then went on a 10-minute tirade, ranting about what a terrible, selfish person I am and how much she hates me. She said I was never a good mother, I am a worthless person and that everyone hates me. All because I said no! I'm afraid of how hateful she will be the next time I see her. I don't even know her anymore. How did you manage??"

In times past, I questioned myself and my sanity when there were flare-ups of this sort. I would rack my brain and try to understand what I did wrong, why I was so worthless, what I could do to fix it. Or I would make the mistake of being lured into defending and explaining myself. We never seemed to get to the bottom of things or reach agreement. Finally, I realized these conflicts don't rise up with fairness and logic; they aren't going to suddenly become fair and logical. Even if we argue until we're out of oxygen. More importantly—**realizing I was dealing with someone whose agenda was to *not* hear me was transformational.**

I will confess, before working on my recovery of peace, I got fed up and gave it right back sometimes, returning vicious for vicious. That is not dignified for anyone.

Backlash against boundaries can be horrendous, especially when first setting them. What a horror when your own child (or any loved one) quickly becomes hateful. I remember the shock of it. We are some years past that now. I'm more than grateful to say I've gone more than 5 years without conflict, dysfunction, or active addiction present in my daily life. The reason I say that is to say this: if you feel caught in an unending cycle of conflict, peace **is** possible. Boundaries do eventually work. At one time my life felt out of control with turmoil and conflict. As much as I know how that feels, I know to a profound degree that *peace is possible.*

Support is crucial. Find support online, or in a meeting, and the sooner the better. Another vital tool is seeking information and education. I remember what a therapist trained in family dysfunction told me: *"Annie, you have to do whatever it takes for* **you** *to be okay, for* **you** *to be safe and at peace. For your environment to be as healthy as possible. Work on how you respond and what you allow. Then life will improve."*

I was also told to remember that as horrendous as it feels, *it's not personal.*

This behavior is par for the course; it occurs with the disease of addiction. **It's not okay**, it's terribly painful and at times traumatizing. But *it's not personal.*

Realizing it's not personal is a hard place to come to and it's definitely a process. It takes time. It *feels* personal. Your personal belongings may become damaged or go missing. Your personal space might be violated. Your personal character can oftentimes be assassinated. But the reality is, the adversarial behavior is not personal.

Years after the fact, when the damage was done, amends had been made, and things had settled, I once asked my son if he meant the things he'd said to me. I asked straightforwardly, "Did you *mean* those things? Did you *think* those things?" His answer was a solid no. "*No,* Mom," he explained, "I had to do whatever it took to get what I needed and get out of the conversation. I was desperate. I wasn't thinking logically. My brain was altered; I was out of control. I couldn't even allow myself to stop long enough to think about how bad you must be feeling, even though deep down I knew it. I was constantly running on sensory overload; your feelings were collateral damage."

Anyone in the path of someone in active addiction is liable to be collateral damage. It's symptomatic. It's not personal. This is why taking care of yourself is vital. Protecting yourself, setting boundaries, and having a plan for the behavior is critical. Over time your healthiness will promote healthiness around you. It's a process; it takes time. When we begin working on our own confidence and worth and stop receiving the vicious words, things started changing. When we handle heated situations with calm, disengaged responses instead of being hyper-reactive, eventually they stop happening.

Going to meetings, getting informed, doing therapy work, calling supportive friends, and taking it day by day all helped bring my life to a more manageable place. After it all, I have learned I can tell this: don't give up hope or give in to despair. It's not personal. *Peace is possible;* it's a process.

Chapter 5

In Times of Crisis, How Do We Fold Laundry or Sit Through a Meeting When Life is Falling Apart?

Continuing on with a daily schedule in the midst of crisis is something we do with a certain amount of emotional auto-pilot.

Often some of the most painful and frightening days of crisis occur when addiction, alcoholism, or SUD come roaring like a tornado through a home and family. I know this type of crisis all too well. I clearly remember days when our lives were extremely chaotic, yet I somehow still needed to focus in work meetings, go to the grocery store, tend to my home, navigate traffic, and keep life demands balanced as much as possible.

Life doesn't stop or even slow down when you're in crisis.

The word **crisis** has three definitions I find particularly interesting...

I.   *Crisis:* **a time of intense difficulty, trouble, or danger.**

"This is the part when you find out who you are." ~ J.H.

When intense troubles arrive, everything dysfunctional within us tends to rise to the surface.

We can find ourselves doing what Author and

Speaker Brené Brown refers to as "chandeliering." Chandeliering is when profound pain or fear causes us to "hit the ceiling" *anytime* we become rattled due to the extreme stress we're under.

What worked best for me in these times was to have tools in place. Some of the work I have done over the years has involved the following:

Trauma Therapy: focuses on post-traumatic stress and grief

Emotion Focused Therapy (EFT): based on methods designed to help people accept, express, regulate, make sense of and transform *emotion.* This method systematically but flexibly helps clients become aware of and make productive use of their **emotions; such as an excessive need to attach, and feelings of paranoia related to perceived rejection or ridicule.**

Cognitive Behavioral Therapy (**CBT**): a short-term, goal-oriented psychotherapy treatment that takes a hands-on, practical approach to problem-solving. Its goal is to change patterns of thinking or behavior that are behind people's difficulties thus changing the way they feel.

Dialectical Behavioral Therapy (DBT): an effective combination of cognitive and behavioral therapies. The goal of DBT is to transform negative thinking patterns and destructive behaviors into positive outcomes.

Most people connect with a therapist in times of turmoil or relationship breakdown not realizing there are specific types of therapy and processes for modifying thoughts, emotions and behaviors. Laymen don't usually know this. Customizing what fits you, your family, and specific circumstances is critical.

I truly believe anyone and everyone would benefit from experiencing or studying therapy. Life is challenging and unpredictable; no one is absolved from trying times.

Once we find some relief in the area of distress and solutions are in place to heal and manage difficult situations, we find life gradually calms and improves. And the good news is we don't unlearn these things. These skills return in future times of crisis when we need them.

* * *

II.   *Crisis:* **a time when difficult or important decisions must be made.**

Interestingly enough, the Greek root word for crisis is *krisis,* which literally means **decision.**

Certainly in times of crisis we are called to turning points of decision. A decision I try to make once I'm aware of a crisis is the choice to grow from it as much as possible versus allowing it to defeat me. While I have absolutely gone through times of Post-Traumatic Stress, those times are not where I prefer to remain. Doing the work to heal forward, I find *Post Traumatic **Growth*** can occur, creating instances of great creativity, new areas of depth, compassion, wisdom, strength, and intense personal development.

Times of crisis tend to peak in strength and intensity. Once we've come down from the "chandelier," it's wise to enter research and action mode next, in order to make smart decisions about handling the situation. This is the time we need to secure support from outside sources, such as crisis intervention agencies, emergency lines, law enforcement if needed, support groups, and therapy, along with trustworthy and **compassionate** friends, family etc.

* * *

III. *Crisis:* **the turning point of a disease when an important change takes place, indicating either recovery or death.**

Often a crisis can be one of the greatest agents for change in our lives. It can be a huge turning point, once we come through the upheaval and shock, and begin to see what and whom it may have led into our lives.

In my opinion, recovery, growth, and triumph in the aftermath of a crisis mean nothing was wasted or without purpose.

In the midst of crisis...

I was trained to ask myself three questions in moments of extreme distress:

"What am I feeling? What can I do? What am I going to do?"

(I kept them on an index card on my desk)

These questions calm the mind in the midst of distress and lead to a productive mindset. We can then apply tools we obtain from therapy, crisis/conflict training, and recovery work, which prompts the next question to ask yourself:

"Am I thinking right?"

We all go into habits of unhealthy, distorted thought patterns when stress or crisis hit. This prevents us from coming to solutions, and can develop into serious defeated, victim-type thinking.

Ten examples of distorted thinking, based on the research of Professor Luckshman Madurassinghe:

Awfulizing: imagining a situation to be fatalistic, worst-case scenario and as bad as it can possibly be. "I awfulized the conversation with my ex-wife, mentally turning it into a nasty confrontation, therefore I opted out of resolving the issue with her."

Tunnel vision (filtering): only one part of a situation is focused on and the rest is ignored. A tendency is to focus on the negative aspects or interpretations of a situation and ignore alternative ways of seeing things. This is when we "can't see the forest for the trees."

All or nothing: splitting our view into extremes; there is no middle ground, everything is either/or. "We are either going to talk this through right now or end up enemies."

Generalizing: making a general or broad statement by inferring from specific cases. "Every person who became addicted happened upon it by making bad choices. They chose their way into addiction, it's always their *fault.*"

Projecting/jumping to conclusions: defending oneself against our own unconscious impulses or qualities (both positive and negative) by denying their existence in ourselves while attributing them to others. We project negative motives into someone without bothering to confirm if we are correct. "He/she is only being manipulative and calculating when they act friendly and warm."

Negativity: the expression of criticism or pessimism about something. "There's *no way* this can work out."

Blame: assigning responsibility for a problem versus working to resolve it. "It's your dad's fault we're struggling like this."

Unfairness: believing there's a lack of equality or justice; an inability to understand that things sometimes will just not work out in our favor. "Why is this happening to **me**? I've been doing all the right things!"

Shoulds: used to indicate obligation, duty, or correctness, typically when criticizing someone's actions. "You *should* have handled that different. You *should* have tried harder. You *should* do this, go here, help this person," etc., etc.

Heaven's reward: we expect our sacrifice and self-denial to pay off, as if someone is keeping score. We feel bitter when the reward doesn't come. "After all I've done for you? After all I've been through...*this* is the thanks I get?"

The truth is, I have personally fallen into just about all of these thought patterns at one time or another, especially in times of stressful conflict or crisis. It wasn't until I experienced therapy, recovery for trauma/codependency, and did research that revealed to me me these even **were** distorted perceptions, that I tried handling situations differently.

No one is immune—we can all fall into unhealthy thinking. Becoming aware of these patterns is key; *adjusting* them going forward is life-changing.

* * *

The last series of questions to ask yourself in crisis is:

"Is this **my** crisis? Did I create the situation and is it something I can, or *need,* to resolve?"

If not, we need to step aside instead of triaging someone else's urgency (which was my usual routine in years past) and tend to what we need to manage within our own life, like the feelings of fear and panic a crisis tends to invoke. This is when we need to breathe, focus, and move through it a moment at a time, before we respond.

Chapter 6

Level 10 Stress

There once was a time when stress for me had two settings only—the needle sat on 0 or it jumped straight to level 10. An unsettling phone call from a loved one could send adrenaline shooting through me as rapidly as if you were to step on the gas and take your car from 0 to 100 mph in 0.3 seconds. I was often hurled into panic. Getting pulled into chaos and the craziness of family conflicts or addiction related crisis was almost a daily event. I know by heart what that's like.

In those days, I was easily snared by gut-wrenching arguments with family members who were enmeshed in our situation. We can also be pulled in by strangers brought across our path by virtue of these circumstances.

When our lives have no peace we quickly find ourselves running on empty.

Returning to 0 between episodes of chaos isn't truly peaceful. Sadness resides in the quiet times, along with fear and dread as we wait for the next wave to crash or more bad news to come.

Emotions can become ferocious alongside the stress. Have you ever tried to wrap your hands around a raging thunder storm or attempted to calm a hurricane? Internally, that's how it felt. The pressure was unbearable, sickening, overwhelming. And yet I had to function through my daily routine.

There is a German saying: *denn wir haben eine Krise der Verzweiflung erreicht*. It translates as:

"For we have reached a crisis of desperation."

Before my son entered recovery over five years ago (and I began to work on recovering my own wellbeing from the long-term effects of the chronic stress), I reached a *crisis of desperation* often. In fact, I did so constantly. Stress and desperation ruled my life; it was the red line, panic zone, miserable kind of stressed-out desperation that rises up with the madness that addiction brings with it. When addiction enters your life it feels as though a freight train comes roaring through the house and keeps coming back! Many times my mind would race wildly and my heart would beat so fast that I would feel my pulse in different places all over my body, throbbing in my temples and neck. Level 10 stress becomes par for the course for a mother, daughter, father, brother, wife etc., who is closely connected to someone in active addiction.

At least at first.

Once you begin seeking recovery, support, and healing, you *will* begin to level out. Somehow once recovery and support enter your life, the crashing-wave moments don't come as often, hit as hard, or last as long.

Crisis and desperation concerning addiction in a family is happening with everyday people who are not expecting to be pulled into profoundly difficult circumstances.

One recent conversation I had was with a shell-shocked mother in a crisis of desperation herself. Only the night before, her son had shaken her awake, whispering and gesturing madly over her, "Mom, wake up!" he ranted frantically. "I need $200, they're waiting outside! Mom, they're going to kill me if I don't pay them! They even said they'll kill *you!*"

This desperate and scared mom once again pulled a handful of cash from a locked safe she'd recently felt the need to purchase for cash and valuables that often went missing.

"This threat is becoming common now!" she told me. "Do I believe it *every* time?" I noticed she sounded as tired as she did worried. "Am I truly to be afraid for his life? Should I fear for my own? Or...do you think maybe he's manipulating me?"

Unfortunately, these insidious situations also sometimes become par for the course for those living with a loved one battling the disease of addiction. These are the moments that send a parent reeling. It feels like you're falling off the world, unable to land. I've been through those intense situations and felt as though fuses were blowing in my brain. It was at times like an out-of-body experience. Sometimes I would get so stressed that I felt like I might start levitating! My brain felt like it was steaming and about to explode. Life became overwhelming. The combination of terror, exhaustion, worry, and sorrow are like a herd of elephants standing on your chest.

So how does one respond? And more than that, how do we go about normal life in the midst of the madness? How do we go in and face a demanding work day when dealing with something so horrendous at home? How can we go to bed, have a fitful night of sleep, and face the *next* day? How do we go to the grocery store, fold the laundry, or ever have a normal, lighthearted conversation with anyone when nothing about life is normal? How can we accomplish a thing while going through this?

Truth be told, it was almost impossible for me at first and it didn't get better overnight. It takes time; it's a process.

While we certainly never want to minimize a threat that could lead to a tragedy, I have learned myself that most of the time in scenarios where money is demanded to avoid physical harm, manipulation absolutely is involved.

Beyond that, I also began to learn that we don't have to jump into the madness and surge along with it. You have to be okay and level-headed to maintain a sane, peaceful, safe environment. Therefore, it's important to develop the ability to not get pulled into the chaos or conflict. I learned that it's actually wise not to.

Living with chronic stress has lasting effects.

Chronic, long-term stress does damage. Brain damage to be precise. Chronic stress actually changes the brain. Long-term stress changes the functions, structure, and size of the brain, according to Madhumita Murgia, in an article appearing in The Daily Telegraph. This information was compiled in a relevant report for TEDx.

Chronic stress literally changes who we are.

Medical research shows that stress begins in the Hypothalamus Pituitary Adrenal Axis (HPA Axis which interacts between the brain and the kidneys). When a stressor occurs, the HPA Axis immediately signals the kidneys to release the stress hormone **cortisol**, signaling the body to instant action. This is helpful in moments when we need a boost, like exercise, moments of danger, etc. However, a long term releasing of cortisol caused by chronic stress wreaks havoc on the body and brain. Areas of the brain inevitably become weakened, as does our ability to deal with stress.

The prefrontal cortex is especially affected. This is the control center for concentration, decision making, judgment and social interaction. As a result, fewer brain cells are made, making it more difficult to learn and remember things.

The long term stress caused me to become forgetful, hasty in my decisions, confused, and socially awkward. Even more than usual! I also noticed that during that time of my life I became clumsier.

At the time it became obvious to me that I was heading for a major crash if I didn't get ahead of my stress. We need to develop strength and calm resolve for the ambush, crazy making moments of chaos. There are solutions. There are ways to handle those stressful moments when cortisol is activated.

There are also ways to reverse the damages.

What I found to be helpful for me in moments of chaos was stepping back, maybe going into another room and closing the door, even if demands were still being aggressively made. Stepping away gives you a moment to collect yourself and not jump into the volatility. I would then take a moment to silently lift the burden off myself and place it onto my Higher Power. Turning it over to my faith, praying "Please help us. Show me what to do. I believe You make all things possible, please make peace possible in the midst of what right now feels like insanity."

Peace always comes, we can feel quiet relief in those moments.

Another method I use when pulled into urgency is to allow myself four deep, full breaths. Deep breathing floods oxygen to our extremities and calms us enough to think about our options. This breathing technique never fails to calm the mind.

If a longer break from the situation is possible, go for a quick walk, drive, bike ride, or run.

If the situation is still surging, you may need outside help and support. This is when we need to call upon a trusted friend. If it *continues* to escalate and we feel it is necessary, contact law enforcement. We should do whatever we feel will be helpful to restore sanity, peace, and safety to our environment.

Something I learned to stop doing was allow those moments to force me to a quick decision.

When you start to respond rationally instead of accelerating with the situation, you'll begin to actually sense yourself calming down in the midst of it. I found that the atmosphere around me would then grow more relaxed as well. Over time, life became more calm and manageable. Addiction, terror and chaos no longer called the shots.

From efforts to improve and recover, I've learned that eventually thicker skin and cooler heads do prevail.

Again, this wasn't easy. It took time and effort. It is definitely a process. Sometimes we'll fail, but we'll get stronger. When we are determined to have a peaceful, sane life, we'll keep working toward it.

*You will not receive your reward without **refusing** to quit.*

As far as undoing the damage, it was noted in the TEDx report that **exercise** and **meditation** are two of the most effective ways of reversing cortisol damage, as they involve deep breathing and mindfulness. It doesn't mean we have to start spending hours in the gym or meditating the morning away! However, these truly are great forms of self-care. I personally try to exercise at least 30 minutes a day, five days a week. I also meditate 10-20 minutes every morning to prepare myself to face the day.

For me, these rituals have boosted my strength and changed my life. **We have to make ourselves a priority.** We can all find 20 minutes here and there for a brisk walk or some other activity to get the blood flowing. And even if it's for only 90 seconds in a quiet room or hallway, pulling away to breathe, meditate, and release pressure will produce great results over time.

It's a process.

These days, we have come so far in that area that I barely remember what those moments were like. That is how permeating peace can be. Not only does life begin to settle down and stabilize, but peace can soothe even the *memories* of traumatic days gone by.

The process of recovery leads not only to peace but to the deepest of relief.

If you find yourself pulled into these kinds of moments, know that you are not alone. It is no way to live and is not something anyone should handle alone. Others have been right where you are and have come through to a much better life. There is hope for peace and relief. Reach out for support, send a message, make a call, attend a meeting. There's help and there is hope. We can get control of stress by not letting the stress control us. Peace is possible. No one should bear it alone.

Chapter 7

Worry is a Drama Queen

Have you ever misread the tone or intention of a text message? And…*run* with it? If that were a competitive sport, I'd be on Olympic-medalist level.

For some of us, our internal narrator will take the words right off the screen and translate them as rudely as possible. By the time we speak with the "offending" person our imagination has run through every worst case possible. Maybe even working it all up into a full blown federal case (to the offending party's total confusion).

Remembering that texts and tone are often easy to misunderstand helps soften the translation.

Some of us create storylines if a friend hasn't reached out for a while. We rant to ourselves, "Surely that must mean she has no interest in my life! What a jerk, with friends like these, who needs friends!"

It's happened.

Hoping to interrupt the usual patterns, these days I try to remember instead to be an adult and ask direct questions about intent if I believe we are veering off course. I might even do the old fashioned thing before running with assumptions and give them a call myself. But regardless, from time to time I do catch myself exaggerating a situation. Knowing we all have busy schedules, it's more likely that our friend is managing daily life rather than intentionally blowing us off. Friendship is give and take, it also requires a little more understanding and a lot less expectation.

Silence can be an even greater fuel for assumptions! In silences, we tend to fill up space with conjecture of the person having the worst possible intent. If time drags on, contrived intentions give way to fear that a tragedy might have occurred. Silence can cause us to assume outrageous things and most often the mind will glom onto *the* most fearful, *the* most dreadful of all possibilities.

We've all done it, especially concerning those we care about.

And then...there are the times when I am trying to reach my son. If he doesn't respond within a few hours, without first considering that he may be working, at the gym, or sleeping, I imagine him tied up in the trunk of a car, being driven to another country, and probably calling out for me. My son finds it extremely annoying that I get so outrageous and dramatic about it.

The mind is a useful, brilliant tool, but it is also limited and can be magnetically drawn toward negativity if we're not careful. Particularly when it comes to conjecture and worry. Taking a breath, meditating for a moment or two, or focusing on something else for a while is useful. Turning away from a runaway train of thought with a positive distraction is a great way to reroute worrisome thinking.

Answers will come, it's so much better to instead wait calmly while assuming the best!

When I was very little there were times in the family car as my father was driving, when he would pull into an empty parking lot, let me sit on his lap, have me grab the steering wheel, and convince me I was driving. Yes, I know that wasn't perfectly safe, but that was *many moons* ago and back then we didn't even use seatbelts all the time. Sometimes parents would smoke cigarettes in the car with their kids! Not saying it was okay, but it was a different era.

That said, that's what he did and I loved it. I truly thought I *was* driving. He would let me go along for a while, "steering" the car. "Oh no!" he'd shout, "be careful!" acting as if he was afraid we would wreck.

If any of my siblings were present they would lean forward from the backseat yelling, "Be careful! We're going to crash!" grabbing the headrest behind us. I would hurry to try to force the wheel in the opposite direction to get control. Eventually, my Dad would jerk the wheel left and right, causing the huge station wagon to swerve and jolt even more (mind you this was at less than 10 mph in an empty mall parking lot) before straightening the car and "saving us."

Seeing Dad's hands above mine, I would remember who was truly in control.

The mind can be off and running before we know it, when it concerns a child, our relationships, and life's many pressures. Unless we work to remain mindful and logical, we can find ourselves believing that negativity and disaster are occurring, or imminent! And in a frenzy to control, we may handle things in ways that make them veer and spiral worse. What a profound relief to remember that there are bigger, more capable hands than our own navigating. Even if we *believe* we're steering, in reality we are not.

Life is much easier when we believe a *best*-case scenario in terms of messages, intentions, or in times of silence. Remembering that people aren't always out to get us and that things will happen as they are meant to happen gives us much more peace than when the mind goes off on a tangent.

When we take our hands off the thing and relax, allowing life to happen, we can trust that the Force of good in the universe will always steer us home.

"I wonder how much of what weighs me down, is not mine to carry." ~ *Aditi*

Relax, nothing is under control.

Chapter 8

Silent Treatment

It took a couple of years to come out of the stress of everything that happened during the (almost) 6 years of my son, Elliot's struggle with an addiction to painkillers following an injury in football. For a family going through that, one thing we often don't realize as we find our way forward is that as much as we suffer emotionally, our chemically addicted loved ones might be traumatized by their experience with addiction as well. Due to how it affects us, we don't lend much empathy or understanding to the impact it may have on them. I know I couldn't comprehend it. It didn't register for me at all. I was too blinded by how much it hurt and terrified me.

That is, until I learned a powerful, eye-opening lesson during a bewildering time.

A couple of years into his recovery, Elliot and I had an argument. We rarely argued once our lives calmed down and we really didn't before either. Conflict most often appeared only when he was not doing well. Therefore, when this disagreement quickly became heated, it triggered old worries of my son possibly relapsing. As was par for the course I "relapsed" myself and I relapsed hard. I spiraled out of my emotional sobriety, back down the rabbit hole of fear, worry, suspicion, and shaming comments. Veering off topic, I slipped back into my old pattern of panic, hounding him with questions about his decisions, moods, and of course questioning his sobriety.

I asked questions that at this point (especially since he was no longer a minor) were really none of my business.

For two weeks we locked horns and neither would budge. And then suddenly my son stopped responding. He shut down all communication, severed all contact. For months (five months, six days to be exact, not that I was counting) Elliot wouldn't answer my calls, emails or texts. Every attempt I made to contact him was met with silence. After more than a month went by, I realized it was serious. I was bewildered, and full of sadness and fear over it. I didn't know if Elliot would be restored to me anytime soon, if ever. His last message said "Listen, I'm doing well, you need to focus on how you are doing. Don't call me."

Oof.

And then the silence. Soul-crushing, mind-rattling, heartbreaking silence. Months of it. I know it could have been worse. My son was alive, healthy, and well. It was five months, not five years, and it wasn't forever. We had survived many intensely difficult things before this. But it was still excruciating. It was a brutal, bitter fog. I mourned our regular conversations. A day did not go by that I was unaware of his absence. My heart was broken over it.

It is a complex and difficult thing when you endure silence from a child even if they are grown and gone. You can't seem to dull the ache and confusion. Whether they've cut you off in anger, or they are off somewhere scary and unknown in addiction. Whatever the case may be. That silence is scary and painful.

A friend walked closely through those months with me. We never came up with anything solid to make it less throbbing and horrendous. All we managed to conclude was that I would have to make the time as productive as possible and not give into despair. One afternoon as usual, our conversation turned to exactly how long it had been since Elliot answered my calls. The grief overwhelmed me—I didn't want to answer this question anymore. Sitting beside me quietly she said, "We have to figure out how you can conquer the silence until it's over."

I have to say, I never truly did. I might have occasionally come to terms with it; there were times of acceptance and peace. But before too long, the waves of sorrow and frustration would come back.

During this time, I decided to set some intentions and resolve to stick to them no matter how things felt. The first intention we can establish is to set our heart to not lose hope. This is when we continuously pray for the very best for our absent loved one's life, as much as we pray for our relationship to be restored.

We can also intentionally speak only positives about them and about the future as we hope and pray regularly for a breakthrough.

One night I sat alone looking at some favorite pictures of my son when hot pain seared through my heart, as it would for any mother struggling in an estranged relationship with a child. I was wiping away tears I could never seem to hold back when I thought of him when suddenly a light came on. It occurred to me that I didn't want to be right anymore. I came to understand that beyond the need to be correct, as adults we need to be fair and we need to be kind.

In an instant, my eyes were opened to the fact that I needed to be more understanding of his take on things. Regardless of the past, in any relationship we need to come to a place of mutual understanding.

Sometimes we spend more time right-fighting than listening and connecting on a loving, human level. Oh my goodness what a disservice this will do to any relationship!

Suddenly his silent position made more sense. The pain and anger I had been feeling about it melted away and I understood that my offended son had a perspective of his own. And he had every right to it.

We sometimes become stuck on the pain and aftershock of being in crisis after going through horrible times. How quickly we can return to all the old fears over someone who was once actively addicted using again (which is ultimately the fear of their death). I had let myself get so worked up that I couldn't (or maybe wouldn't) stop to see Elliot's perspective. To be brutally honest, back then it almost didn't occur to me that he had a right to one. My focus was too fixed on what he should be doing along with how it all affected *me*.

It makes me cringe to remember how stubborn my thinking was at the time. As heart-wrenching it was to not hear from my son, I'd still clung to the belief that I was the only one who was right.

Have you ever been so right that you ended up *becoming wrong?*

I would not have imagined that my son, who I felt had caused my misery and fear when he was in the grip of this disease, could himself be wounded and affected by it. Nor did I stop to think that my accusing and questioning was a trigger for him, as much as certain things could spark dormant fear and pain within me. Oh, what a difference understanding and compassion can make. My heart surged with the relief of a breakthrough.

There are times for the greater good when it's critical to *hug the cactus*.

"Hugging the cactus until it no longer hurts" is another way of saying we need to get comfortable facing our flaws until it doesn't hurt anymore to look inward. We need to regard our own inaccuracies and examine our motives and behavior. Introspection is a powerful tool, necessary and healthy for every human relationship—personal or professional.

And just when I reached this place of introspection and compassion...he called.

Thankfully, Elliot and I have since been restored. We are again joyful and healthy in our relationship, if not more balanced by respect and kindness. What a hard lesson to learn, yet I am profoundly grateful for it. I absolutely needed to become more self-aware, as we all do. Stopping to consider where someone else might be coming from can undo a lot of misunderstanding and frustration.

Often we come to the deepest truths in the darkest times. Life is brutal this way as much as it's beautiful. Never give up—you never know what can happen in a day. Eyes can be opened, hearts can be softened, silences can be broken. Relationships can be restored.

Chapter 9

Resisting the Waves: What I've Learned About Despair

I don't know what crushes the heart worse than grief and despair, which always seem to be accompanied by fear. C.S. Lewis once said, *"No one ever told me that grief felt so like fear."*

Grief and fear seem to naturally intertwine, making it difficult to distinguish which is surging harder. They both ebb and flow with sickening strength, sometimes crashing in out of nowhere, relentlessly bombarding when one is in a season of loss or upheaval.

My first season of despair came by way of a divorce that happened to occur adjacent to the hospitalization and death of my father. There were many times I would leave my dad's bedside in the palliative wing of the hospital during his last days, rush to the courtroom to face attorneys and divorce proceedings, and then on to pick my son up from school. We would then drive back to hospice to sit beside my father. I would often stare off into space and marvel that this could possibly be my life. Misery seemed to come from all sides.

Fear for the future was overwhelming. How would we survive in the aftermath of so much loss and heartache? I was dumbfounded as to how to explain to my young son that life would feel normal again.

One day at a time, we got through it.

The next round of despair came as a shock. Ten years after my father's death, grief and fear hit like a speeding train when, following an injury and resulting opiate dependency, my son Elliot spiraled through darkness to find his way to recovery, pulling my heart alongside him.

Five years after going through the crisis of addiction, Elliot moved across the country to pursue health, recovery, and a new life of adventure. A brand new grief set in, that of missing him and having an empty, quiet home.

Grief and fear continue to veer in and out of my life even if imminent danger is at bay for the time being. Those emotions can be ferocious. More so when we struggle against them.

On a side note, I've never had a consistently close, healthy relationship with my mother. However, like in any relationship, there were good times and even some very special moments I'll always treasure. One such moment was when I was wrestling with my broken heart during the long, quiet days after my divorce was final and my father died.

My mother pulled a chair beside my bed one evening when I was overwhelmed with sadness and she sat silently for a long time. Finally, she told me, "When your heart is broken, misery hits like a crashing ocean wave." She went on to say that when we struggle against it, we only invite it to hit harder and last longer. "Try instead to accept the wave when it hits. Tell yourself: 'Yeah, I'm miserable right now' and then just be with the misery. It will pass and soon you find that the waves don't crash nearly as hard or come as often. Before you know it, they rarely come back at all."

I took her advice and met my grief and despair with

acceptance every time the waves returned. Before too long, I found myself getting through them to a place of peace instead of being crushed under the weight.

Author Neil Strauss in a blog post titled "A Big Misconception about Happiness" speaks of a similar way of looking harsh emotions: "Don't resist the emotions you perceive as negative–resistance makes them stronger. Try Acceptance. You'll find that if you accept an emotion, it begins to lose its power over you."

He goes on to say his two-year-old son doesn't resist emotions—he faces them fully. And once they're over, they're gone.

Emotions have less power over us when we face strong feelings head-on, with acceptance and a determination to press through.

Feelings come and go, rise and fall, they appear and they subside. Resisting, denying, avoiding, or attempting to numb them will only postpone peace.

I find my way to acceptance much easier by calling upon the Source of my faith. The Force in the universe made of love and goodness. The One who is for me, not against me. Always helping, always aware, always present. It is God who grants me the serenity to accept the things I cannot change, the courage to change the things I can, and the wisdom to know the difference.

Chapter 10

Arguing with an Addicted Loved One is Like Reasoning with a Hurricane

There are more people *affected* by addiction than addicted. It's been said that for every one person struggling with addiction, there are at least 15 people affected. The effects are painful and relentless for those of us suffering on the sidelines. Affected family members feel helpless about changing the situation. We stand by, most often totally sober and aware, knowing that addiction is capable of quickly devouring people right before our eyes.

It's no secret that addiction has ripped its way through my home and family. At least not since my book *"Unhooked, a Mother's Story of Unhitching from the Roller Coaster of Her Son's Addiction"* was published. *Unhooked* details my tumultuous struggle with my mother as well as a six-year journey through the prescription-pill addiction of my son and only child following an injury in football. I have been in the presence of active addiction my entire life; it is an ordeal I wish on no one. Like many, I have not lived a single day of my life unaffected by someone's addiction and/or addiction-related behavior. Not one day. Navigating my way through life with this affliction present, always lurking and often rearing its head with great velocity, has been an emotional obstacle course.

One of the ways we might find ourselves pulled into a

struggle with the insanity and dysfunction of addiction is when "bottomless arguments" flare up. Particularly those that involve a combination of deceptive tactics.

When arguments arise and become excessively heated, seem unsolvable and involve dynamics like **blame-shifting**, **denial,** and **false accusation,** I personally believe we are most likely in the presence of active addiction, relapse, or some other deception that desperately wants to stay hidden. I've found the stronger these tactics are applied by the person I am in the struggle with, the deeper the deception.

I will elaborate. The following are behaviors I have personally experienced during times I've found myself in conflict with someone I care greatly about, but who struggles with the infirmity of addiction.

Blame-shifting: *a tactic used to push blame onto another. The act of transferring responsibility for an error or problem to another person.*

In my experience, the best of manipulators will apply this form of emotional abuse. It's a slippery, shirking, somewhat "juking" way of side-stepping ownership for decisions and behavior. Whatever the offending party is confronted with, it is *always someone else's fault.* Something or someone *caused* them to behave as they did. As if they are puppeteered against their own will, when in fact these are often very strong-willed people who can't be *forced* to do a thing we'd like them to!

It's best to refuse to go deep into conversation with blame-shifting. Set that boundary firmly. As soon as you recognize it, back out of the conversation and respond to the blame-shifting *independently* and internally.

A few modified approaches might include:

- Walking your dog to take a breather
- Praying or meditating for 10 or 15 minutes
- Calling a trusted friend in your support system
- A few yoga stretches or 20 jumping jacks

These are all ways to clear frustrated energy and remove ourselves from an argument that's going nowhere.

Blame-shifting is an abusive, conniving tactic that, very simply put, distracts from accountability, addressing the truth, and problem solving.

Denial: *refusing to admit the truth or reality.*

Addiction is never alive and well without the presence of denial. Denial is malleable; it takes on many forms. A person who is unwilling to face, or admit, the truth will go to the death fighting to deny it. Another version of denial is family members desperate not to believe the whispers of truth that have been alerting them all along. Family members frequently resist believing that the ominous situation that they're afraid of, is actually happening.

I tend to be one who dives right into the truth, just as I prefer jumping into a swimming pool versus inching my way in to slowly get used to the cold water. Facing reality head-on gets it over with more quickly and allows us to begin making decisions toward solutions.

That said, having a person who holds weight in your life refuse to admit that a situation is happening—even in the presence of proof—is one of the most frustrating experiences. Before one becomes knowledgeable about the tactics of someone addicted (who will do anything they can to protect the anonymity of their problem), it's easy to get swept up by the hurricane of distracting behavior.

I myself have been lured into the storm too many times to remember. Many times I would even invent brand new, intricate ways of catching lies that would put CIA agents to shame. All without stopping to think:

Wait, maybe I could just...not go down this rabbit hole. Maybe this isn't even my fight. Perhaps I don't have to run this race or step into this storm. Instead, I could calmly realize that if things are not adding up, clearly something is wrong and I should remove myself from the chaos rather than being caught in it. I need to instead set consistent, firm, healthy boundaries and settle on the fact that if I am right, the truth will expose itself eventually. What use is it to work this hard to nail down a confession? Have I forcefully proven one point so far that caused things to turn around? What can I do if I am right? The person denying the truth will just get better at disguising it next time.

To a degree, searching for answers is a must, but just like a song plays itself out on the radio...at some point I know when that tune has had its run. I cannot walk in the kindest, healthiest version of myself if I am in a long, drawn-out dogfight to expose something. At some point I have to step back and allow nature to take its course.

Truth always comes out eventually. What a relief.

"In wartime truth is so precious that she should always be attended by a bodyguard of lies." ~ *Winston Churchill, The Second World War,* Volume V: *Closing the Ring,* Boston, Houghton Mifflin, 1951, p. 383

Through the years, my afflicted mother and I have had knock-down, drag *out* fights of epic proportion over her unwillingness to admit the truth. It's happened more times than I care to confess. It always started the same: an offending (sometimes dangerous) situation would come to my attention. My first attempt to address it would be calm as I carefully confronted her. Because I am stubbornly optimistic, I always believed that *this time* the outcome would be fair and good. I would painstakingly plan how to approach her just in case I actually *was* the trigger for her lies and denial, which she usually blamed me for; if she lied, it was "because I forced her to, I gave her no choice." (Denial and blame-shifting very often work as a team).

I would tread lightly to give her every opportunity to be honest, promising I was on her side and not coming at her in anger even though most things I confronted her about were clearly wrong and often outrageously unsafe. The issue at hand—whether it was interfering with my son, keeping dangerous secrets that as a parent I needed to know, her unpredictable lying, or unlawful use of narcotic prescription pain medication — was immediately lied about. Denial. It will be the knee-jerk, first-instinct response for someone in active addiction.

Because of a dependency to prescriptions that began innocently long ago, my mother has lied to my face with a Bible on her lap. I came to understand that she was pulled deep into deception by her disorder. The madness of it just about cost me my mind and more than once cost me my temper.

But long before I would lose my temper, I first tried to present the evidence with reasoning and fact. In response, she'd escalate the denial and add heat to it by talking faster and sidestepping the issue with reasons her life has been hard. She would even tell me her life has been *too hard for this conversation.* As insane as it was, this part could last over an hour. I would allow her to spin me all over the place with distracting complaints and excuses. When I would finally pin her down with too much truth to deny, she would flip her script and get mean, accusing me of things that were outrageous. It was just a nasty spewing of vitriol. I was guilty also, as I would then respond with the same spewing of venom.

Vitriol can be described as a bitter rant of hate-filled criticism. A brand of sulfuric acid was named Vitriol, reason being that the acid was strong enough to burn through any type of material, including steel and rock.

Another permanent boundary to set: **do not remain in the presence of vitriol.**

My mother, like any desperately ill, addicted person, is very hard to pin down on any one point. She spins left and veers right like a seasoned quarterback. This would cause me to chase down one distracting thing after another. The closer we get to exposing a truth with someone sick with addiction, the harder they'll fight.

The disrupted mind of an addict will not stay on task. When you are locked into this type of dispute, you may find yourself listening to a spewing of lies describing what a terrible person/parent/partner/ child *you* have been—in response to asking fair questions about things they are *truly* guilty of. It all seems backwards, upside down and, in all honesty, can be crazy-making! These are tactics they are using to distract, absolve themselves of guilt, and avoid accountability. Active users are great at manipulating, distracting, and justifying; that is how they get by. It's worth knowing that in the meantime they are also avoiding telling *themselves* the truth.

When in this cycle, someone actively using will fight their way out of taking responsibility. Often going to any length to avoid admitting that a single decision they are making is their fault.

In a way, that's true—the disease of addiction is

calling the shots.

Active users who are deep into the disease will lie and confuse in layers. But there is one central truth rooted deep within it all: that truth is that **they are addicted**.

That is the problem within every problem. Those afflicted with addiction *have* to lie. They have to justify. They have to blame. It's how (they believe) they have to survive. To begin talking in truths, to start taking responsibility for their decisions would begin an unraveling of the layers that cover up the central deception. They can't do it. They won't—they're not ready. The disease still has a hold.

For those of us who are affected, it's like trying to argue with a hurricane.

If I've learned anything it is this: *never* **argue with a person in active addiction. Arguments are their comfortable playing field. You'll get lured in, hooked with the hope of resolution yet quickly find yourself confused, accused, devoured, and enraged beyond your norm.**

Instead of trying to get a storm to negotiate, I know now to take cover. Take care of yourself and put your trust in your Higher Power to calm the storm. You don't have to go through it anymore. There is no reasoning with a hurricane. As boundaries remain firm and consistent, life has to be handled totally different when addiction is present.

If you are related to, living with, or dealing in any way with someone you know or suspect is active in addiction, the crucial thing is to take care of you. A healthy you is healthier for everyone. Addiction causes havoc and destruction in any setting. Trying to argue, prove, manage, or reason with addiction is like shouting at a raging tidal wave—there is no possible way to maneuver it. The wise thing to do is take cover, find calm and peace for yourself, and keep your boundaries firm. You can deal with the damage once the storm has passed over, *if you so choose.*

What a relief!

False accusation (I've heard it described it this way): *A false allegation can occur as the result of intentional lying on the part of the accuser, or unintentionally, due to a confabulation (a false memory used to fill in gaps), or when a person is suspected of a wrongdoing for which the accusing party is actually in fact responsible. False accusations may be used to divert attention from one's own guilt.*

Additionally, once a false accusation has been made— particularly an emotionally laden one—normal human emotional responses to being falsely accused (such as fear, anger, or denial of the accusation) may be interpreted as evidence of guilt.

For me this is the most frustrating tactic to navigate. It can seem as though the more you try to set things straight the less believable you appear.

My Dad taught me years ago that if I ever lost control driving a car on ice, to let go of the steering wheel. He told me to do it long enough for the car to straighten itself out. I have also found this to be my best strategy when it comes to false accusations. Sometimes we just have to take our hands off, go silent, hold onto our peace while knowing the truth, and trust that it will straighten itself out.

Eventually it will—truth always comes out. In the meantime, the harder we try to steer our way through it, the worse it can feel like its spiraling out of control.

"If you tell the truth it becomes part of your past. But a

lie becomes part of your future." ~Unknown

Those who lie, accuse, and condemn are not trying to find peace and solution. They are not coming from a healthy place—they are most often hiding a deception or an addiction. Accusation and condemnation are not methods of healthy accountability or problem solving. They are no more than distractions and no less than dysfunction.

When someone with a pattern of addiction and untrustworthiness begins accusing us it's easy to wonder, "How is it that *I'm* in the hot seat? This makes no sense!" And it's never going to.

We will never come up with enough evidence, correct words, or a strong enough defense for peace or truth to break through when we are in this place with someone. And so it goes with the disease of addiction. There is no arguing with an active user. They don't fight fair. They don't want solution and peace. They want to "feel well" (get high) and they have to keep the lies covered up in order to do so.

For years this was my private horror story that I shared with very few. That is, until I chose to step out of the pathology of dysfunction, depart from our norm, and find new ways of coping.

When my son fell into the plight of prescribed addiction after an injury, I finally chose to begin seeking support and recovery. I felt my son's life depended upon *my* strength and sanity. Valuing his life forced me to finally value my own.

In spite of my mother's illness and so much resulting conflict, one fact I also had to face was that I had a part in it all. I, too, participated in the cycles of madness in my obsessive efforts to fight for what I believed was right, true, and fair. On my side of the street, I was fighting just as viciously to be heard, for facts to be seen, and for behaviors to stop. All the while things got worse because I was, in fact, fighting a losing battle with a chemical addiction versus trying to reason with a healthy, rational adult.

That was a long, slow, painful conclusion to come to, because this was my *mother*. This was my mom we're talking about. It felt impossible to accept that I would never have the final, breakthrough conversation with her that would result in a healthy relationship for us or at the very least simply bring us to a *peaceful* place.

Facing the truth was slow, complex, and it felt terrible...but it set me free.

I don't have to have those conversations of torment anymore. I don't have to hang up the phone and call a friend in tears asking if I'm crazy and possibly seeing it all wrong. To be peaceful and free we have to work to see things not as we hope they can be, but for how they *are*.

Just as one would not likely walk into a loud, rowdy bar at "last call" to try to argue with someone who has been drinking whiskey all day, we cannot argue with a person deep in substance abuse.

If you recognize any of these behaviors or tactics occurring in your own life, know that you are not alone. It takes work but you too can find peace in the midst of the storm. Walk away, meditate, find a recovery support group (online or face to face meetings), call a friend, take 90 seconds to breathe, and then return to the conversation *if you must*. You have options for hope and relief! And always—you can turn it all over to Your Higher Power who is better able to handle it than you or I will ever be. You can trust the process. What a relief.

"Let there be
an opening
into the quiet
that lies beneath
the chaos,
where you find
the peace
you did not think
possible
and see what shimmers
within the storm."
~Jan Richardson

Chapter 11

PTSD: Do You Have It? Is it Permanent?

All my life I've been the type to pull myself up by the bootstraps and go on. No matter *how* terrible things felt. But there have been occasions when I knew I needed to sit down in the midst of a mess to regroup and regain my balance.

A few years ago, having gone through turmoil related to conflict, dysfunction, and addiction within my family (as well as other distressing circumstances that occurred simultaneously, because **"when it rains it pours!"**), I was given a vague diagnosis of having Post-Traumatic Stress Disorder by my family physician. Being skeptical, I then had it confirmed by a psychologist.

Some of us experience the *complex* version (C-PTSD) which occurs as a result of repetitive and extreme stress over a prolonged period of time, versus resulting from a traumatic one time incident.

Of course I was stressed out and frazzled. More than anything else I was managing, I was the mother of a son who had just been through a life and death struggle. Though our lives had calmed down, I was so affected that I couldn't seem to control the terror, anxiety, and worry that remained. Trauma tends to derail emotional regulation.

You are never quite the same after an experience like that.

I was handed a list of suggestions for how to manage it and went home to sort it out. Being a student of life and adversity, I decided to look deep into the condition and figure out how to come through it triumphantly.

What are causes, signs and symptoms of PTSD?

We've all heard of PTSD; a disorder that can develop in people who have experienced traumatic, shocking, scary, or dangerous events. But what does it really *mean* to have it and what are possible causes?

Trauma can mean many things. It's defined as "a deeply distressing or disturbing experience; an experience that produces extreme psychological stress, injury, or pain."

Symptoms of this condition include flashbacks, bad dreams, and frightening thoughts that may begin in the person's mind or appear when memories are triggered.

Other signs of PTSD and C-PTSD are being hyper-alert, easily aroused or startled, feeling on edge, having difficulty sleeping, and experiencing angry outbursts. We also might sink into low self-esteem, isolation, and lose interest in enjoyable activities.

If not tended to, these symptoms can gain momentum and lead to depression and even thoughts of suicide.

A normal next question is...

Is PTSD permanent?

Some experiences are so distressing that any reminder of them can cause us to **revivify** the situation, and we can become **trauma stuck**.

Once we get stuck on an injury, we relive it over and over, whether triggered or not. This is called ruminating; when one dwells on prior events, mentally replaying them and filtering *present* situations negatively through a *past* experience.

There's hope!

I don't know about anyone else, but when I'm stuck on anger, pain, or bitterness I experience *no* new development in my life. I don't grow, it's difficult to hear and learn, I don't fully participate in all life has for me, and I certainly can't experience fullness of joy and peace.

We will stay stuck right there until we set an intention to move on.

Trauma and PTSD are not impossible, or even that complicated to work through. How much healthier it is to do the uncomfortable work versus remaining stuck in old injuries, not moving forward with life.

A huge part of the solution is becoming aware that we're stuck.

The next step is *acknowledging* it. Speak to a trustworthy friend, adviser, or counselor. There is relief in laying the truth out bare. It's humbling and scary, but it brings *relief.*

And then, we need to do something about it!

Find support.

If the trauma is still occurring, it's even more crucial to have a strong support system and tools for coping in place.

Support groups, recovery meetings, therapy, classes, workshops, and therapy workbooks are all great tools and are easily available. Don't suffer alone or sit forever in the stress and struggle. It doesn't just go away. We have to be proactive for our health and emotional/mental well-being.

Even years past our crisis, there are still moments when I feel a surge of fight-or-flight adrenaline because a memory is triggered. *Especially* if it relates to my son.

That's the time to turn to a helpful resource, work through it, and find peace.

* * *

I believe *nothing* matters more than health. Health isn't just the physical aspect. Wellness includes our mental and emotional condition. We often see people post healthy meals or workouts on social media. While physical health is absolutely vital, if we're not mentally and emotionally sound as well, we're not as strong as we think we are.

Our lives can collapse like a house of cards without the full trifecta of wellness. We need emotional and mental health more than we openly acknowledge.

(That doesn't mean we have to post a selfie while meditating, pouring over a counseling workbook, or from a therapist's couch. But doing mental and emotional exercises to alleviate distress caused by upsetting events *is as important* as watching calorie intake and having a strong cardio routine, if not more.)

* * *

Post Traumatic *Strength Development*

We can be determined to **not** get stuck in PTSD. That does not mean denying and avoiding painful issues. We absolutely have to allow ourselves to melt down, grieve, vent, fume, process through, and recover. That time is critical. At some point after that, we need to heal forward from grievous experiences. At least I do.

As much as is written about PTSD, not a lot is said about **growth** after trauma.

This is what I call "**Post Traumatic Strength Development**." This is the newfound strength and progress that comes after crisis.

We're never the same after crisis, but when we have faced adversity and worked it through, we can actually become stronger and empowered by what happened.

A new strength I discovered is being at ease about my history. I used to have intense fear of opening up about things that occurred in my life, out of concern that people would ridicule or shun me. But as a result of all my family has been through and the intense work I've done to recover, I no longer care. I now openly share without a second thought. I'm not intimidated by potentially rude, negative responses. Anyone who shames and mocks others has their own issues to recover from, and that's not for me to be concerned with. There can be great reward from adversity for those who are timid and withdrawn.

I may not share what's happening in my private life at the moment, but once something has been dealt with, I freely share what I've come through, how I made peace with it, and what I've learned. This is in an effort to encourage others who might feel as alone in their struggle as I did. Our service to others is where healing is made concrete.

Five years ago my heart would've melted at the thought of that.

Another example is that for years I had what I called "Doormat Syndrome." At any given time, someone was usually taking advantage of me, trying to bully me, or both.

Some of us magnetically attract these situations.

Trauma attracts drama. I rarely dealt with it in healthy ways. Reason being—I felt I'd been through so much dysfunction, surely I was worthless. Which meant I also felt worth **less** than anyone else. I believed I was too damaged to matter.

My patterns of dysfunction tend to be self-disdaining, rather than taking advantage of, or abusing anyone else.

When your thought patterns run along these routes, you sometimes believe that most negative things that happen around you are your fault, including the mistreatment and misbehavior of others. Ever had anyone treat you disrespectfully and blame you for it? Or maybe you blame yourself? Thinking you caused it or *deserve* it?

I **lived** in that mindset. It's a dead-end, discouraging way to think. We can be captive to it for years.

Not only did I believe many distortions of truth, I was completely obsessed and paralyzed by the stressful condition of my family.

Realistically, when you are stuck in that space, you *can't* put energy into combating anything else. I had little mental or emotional energy to battle anything or anyone other than my own crises, pathology, and *monstrous* heartache.

Internally that puts us all over the place. Outwardly I worked very hard to take care of everything around me and keep my suffering to myself. Can you relate?

Nevertheless, when we start seriously doing the work to recover, all of that dysfunction can be cleaned out in the process. As my confidence, dignity, and self-respect became whole, my mind found peace. This is the hope and promise of therapy and recovery at work.

I am happy to say the doormat days are far behind me.

Along with all that mess being over, I'm no longer easily fooled, manipulated, or backed into a corner, which were relentless patterns in my life. Nor do I allow stress to build to a raging inferno within, causing me to overreact about something insignificant.

Recovery work heals it all.

* * *

Unafraid

After the trauma it can be as if we truly wake up.

I now live life open-minded, with an unafraid, welcoming heart. I take more risks, give very little emotion to the opinions of those not close to me. I set new goals on a weekly basis and I *tell* those I care about how much they matter.

These are all things that get lost in the shuffle of anxiety and a dreary mindset.

After going through so much darkness, including the *primal* fear and despair that comes with the crisis of family addiction (and the sorrow of feeling alone and hopeless in it), finding my way to health and wholeness has been for me like a second chance at life.

A new outlook makes you want to celebrate something about life daily. Even on the not so great days. Wholeness.

When we *do the work* for ourselves, **PTSD is not permanent.**

As much as I had all signs and symptoms of (C) PTSD, I now have all of the **benefits** of *Post Traumatic Strength Development.*

Trauma and recovery change our lives forever.

I wouldn't choose to go through it again, nor would I wish those days on *anyone*, but I wouldn't change what's in my history.

PTSD (even when complex) is *not permanent*.

And if new traumas happen, support and tools are in place to better handle them. Wellness. Not only can life *post*-trauma be good again, it can become better than before.

Chapter 12

Am I Enabling?

The word "enabling" has become almost a curse word for those dealing with a loved one who struggles with addiction. Enabling is a worthwhile subject to look into closely.

One definition of enabling is: **to give someone the authority or means to do something. To make possible.**

It's been some years since our lives were personally turned upside down by the epidemic of addiction that is sweeping our nation. But in the midst of the turmoil, enabling versus *not* enabling were recurring conversations in my home.

I read and researched everything I could find on the subject of addiction in order to play the hand we were dealt correctly and not enable my son into a jail cell or an early death.

As do the majority of parents, I believed with all my heart that the responsibility of curing my son of this disease lay solely upon me and my ability to *not* enable. I eventually learned this was not the truth. While we can contribute in negative or positive ways and influence the situation, we cannot orchestrate a specific outcome.

It's worth knowing that the healthiest position to remain in is one that encourages and empowers versus enabling. Because addiction is not an individual crisis—it is a family disorder that affects and involves every person in its orbit. Without mindful recovery work and self-examination, we will all in some way participate in the problem in our own dysfunctional ways. We all play a role.

One baseline truth is that stepping in to prevent someone from experiencing a negative consequence actually robs them of a life lesson they need to learn or an accomplishment they can take pride from.

Signs you might be enabling

- Ignoring negative or potentially dangerous behavior: This can involve anything from overlooking problems to denying that a problem even exists.

- Difficulty expressing emotions: Enablers are often uncomfortable expressing their own feelings, especially if there are negative repercussions for doing so.

- Prioritizing another's needs before our own: While it is natural to want to help loved ones, enabling takes helping a step too far. Usually the addicted loved one has his/her needs taken care of while the enabler neglects their own.

- Acting out of fear: Since addiction can cause frightening events, the enabler will do whatever it takes to avoid such situations.

- Lying to others to cover behavior: An enabler will lie to keep the peace and to present a controlled, calm exterior that things are just fine.

- Blaming people or situations other than your loved one: to protect them from the consequences of drug abuse, the enabler might accuse other people of *causing* drug abuse or somehow being in the wrong

- Resenting the person you are helping: The result of the above behaviors is that the enabler will likely feel angry and hurt. She/he may act on these feelings by resenting the addict all while continuing to enable the addiction.

- Continuing to help when help is not appreciated or acknowledged.

If these questions make you realize you might be engaging in unhealthy enabling, it is important to take positive action. If the struggling person you believe you are enabling is working on recovery, you too should take part in a process. If that person is not in treatment or working on recovery, you should explore your own issues, either with a personal counselor or through a helpful organization such as Nar-Anon, Alateen, Al-Anon, or one of the many other supportive communities now available. The goal is to be a part of the solution, not a contributor to the problem.

Concepts taken from the Anatomy of Addiction, Psychology Today and Foundations Recovery blog

Breaking the cycle of enabling:

- Leave messes as they are.

- Weigh the options of short-term versus long-term pain (will helping one more time cause more pain in the long run? Cause future demands and pressure?) and interrupt the pattern.

- Get your back autonomy (freedom and independence) and don't allow yourself to be put in danger or dragged along for the ride.

- Develop consistency, consistent standards, and boundaries.

Sometimes we believe handling things a certain way

gives us control of the outcome. We think remaining involved will block a loved one's downfall or even prevent their death.

This all comes back to our own fear and need to control. Our own buried needs to feel safe and comfortable versus what is best for our loved one and the relationship we have with them.

It can take a while to realize that we really control nothing. In fact, anyone we try to control ends up having control over us.

Does *not* enabling resolve addiction?

Isn't that what we've been trained to believe? The moment we put our foot down, our loved will hit that rock bottom and magically find recovery. Problem solved!

But not only is that *not* the case, this thinking deceives us into believing we are in control of their decisions and can orchestrate their journey. While we can contribute in good or bad ways, not enabling by no means resolves the destructive cycle.

In fact, when we step aside and stop enabling, someone else is often next in line to make the behavior possible.

The best rule of thumb when making a decision concerning helping another is to do what is best to feel safe, sane, and at peace. Don't say no because you think you might be negatively enabling while feeling tortured inside because you really wanted to say yes.

By the same token, don't say yes to helping because you believe it will effect an outcome, control someone's decision to pursue recovery, or cause them to act loving toward you again.

Let your yes be yes and your no be no, and make sure your answers are backed up by *your* own peace of mind.

Helping versus enabling

Having a bottom line to stick with helps us have clear thinking when it comes to enabling. As much as you are able and at peace with, it is human and kind to help bear another's burdens. But we are not called to shoulder another's load.

No one is meant to carry another adult's responsibilities, do things for them that *they* are able to do, undo consequences that they need to deal with, or clean up messes we did not make. This is part of the sickness.

When we find we are doing any of the above, we'll start to feel weighed down, worn out, and often resentful.

Enabling involves pressure and demand and causes us to take on problems we are not meant to solve. If you solve someone's problems, chances are you will have to do it again...and again. At some point we grow weary of the cycle. Helping on the other hand, doesn't hinder progress. Helping should feel effortless, absent of turmoil and negativity, void of fear and control.

Along the journey, pray for the wisdom to know the difference.

Chapter 13

What I Learned About Relapse

Equanimity: *Mental calmness, composure, and evenness of temper, especially in a difficult situation.*

I am the mother, daughter, relative, and friend of someone who has struggled with addiction. Like many who hear about, or personally experience the ravaging effects of addiction, it took some serious convincing for me to totally consider it a "disease." In fact, I was pretty self-righteous about it. Like many, I told myself you don't see a cancer patient or diabetic stealing from the jewelry box of a family member or doing things to hurt the people who love and care about them. The truth is, I didn't have an informed understanding of it. I was certain I could outsmart and consequence my son and other loved ones out of addiction. I was the sharp tongued, correct-handling, consequence-forcing, perfect model of a non-enabler. Some of us can be a hard sell when it comes to seeing addiction as a disease that we are powerless over.

Similar to how someone diagnosed with a heart condition needs to make serious lifestyle changes, an addicted person must renovate their entire life in order to arrest and recover from the diseased thinking and cravings that began with the choice to pick up their particular substance in the beginning. Brain chemistry changes once someone becomes gripped and that is often innocently done, based on injury or falling under influence. It can and it does happen

91

to anyone. With dependency upon chemicals, brain chemistry becomes disordered, causing desperation and the need to bypass the love of family and often ethics. People raised to know better can become deceptive and even criminal, needing their next fix as much as their lungs need oxygen. It is only the addicted person who can choose to take the road to recovery. We can affect that path to a degree, but we cannot control it.

I have never understood this more than after witnessing a relapse.

My son went into recovery five years ago but had two relapse setbacks, each with a worse set of circumstances. Once we as a family start to get our lives back on track after addiction hits and a struggling loved one begins to recover, a relapse can feel more crushing than when we found out they were addicted to begin with. This is because when they agree to head to treatment, we want to believe it means they've sobered up once and forever. While not always, unfortunately relapses are sometimes part of the recovery journey.

When it happens, though it stings terribly, it is not about you and it's not a direct shot against you. *Addiction* is not about you and it's not about me. It's not a personal attack. Relapse is about the fact that the disease is chronic and recovery has to be consistent and taken serious every day. If we all live through it and consequences aren't too damaging, much can be learned from a relapse.

The most valuable thing we can learn is how to separate our peace of mind and detach our core sense of well-being from someone else's roller coaster. Sure there will be triggers, which can be painful and terrifying. But we don't have to live in the ups and downs, or run alongside the craziness of anyone else's choices.

In the midst of my son's scariest relapse, I stepped out of the storm. I found my own peace and serenity and discovered what has become my favorite word. **Equanimity**. We can compare equanimity to trying to do a quiet activity like read, take a nap, pray, or meditate while a loud jackhammer tears up the sidewalk outside your window. With practice and discipline, we can learn how to calm ourselves and separate from the noise and chaos as it's happening. It *is* possible! But it takes a decision and time.

Often when an afflicted loved one calls in a panic over problems or stress, our mind will begin to triage the issues for them, almost like a reflex, instead of considering the fact that maybe we're not *supposed* to handle it. Very counter intuitive for a parent or someone with an inner drive to "fix" problems! But when you are dealing with the disease of addiction, life has to be handled completely different. We can't jump into the stress with them. You can love someone without taking on their problems—in fact that is what's healthiest.

After the relapse I took more classes and learned additional ways of handling my role as an affected family member. I returned to my stress management tools and reread notes of helpful ways to handle crisis moments.

Another thing I learned after the relapse was to fully lean on the *The 3 C's of Nar Anon:*

*You didn't **Cause** it, you can't **Control** it, you can't **Cure** it.*

Cause: At this point blaming who, what, where, why and how the addiction started is futile. That only adds to the misery and distracts from handling it in functional, healthy ways. This pertains to past and present as much as the potential substance abuse. Don't live in fear and think that by saying/doing the wrong thing you will send them spiraling back into the cycle. You are not the cause of that. Someone who wants to remain clean will do so regardless of stress or pressure. There will always be stress and pressure! The key is learning to cope without abusing a substance, and that is up to them to develop. Emotionally tiptoeing around someone won't prevent substance abuse any more than bulldozing or bullying will. Working a program is the way forward. You take care of you. Your priority is to make sure **you** are healthy and functional.

Control: Policing and making sure they are going to meetings, spending time with sober companions, doing all they're supposed to, should only be things you pay attention to for your own safety and boundaries. Babysitting another adult's life and recovery, or trying to prevent a setback is not healthy for anyone.

Cure: Nothing you can do, say, think, or feel will heal or cure your loved one's addiction. You can affect their decisions with healthy boundaries and responses by not enabling use or participating in negative, dysfunctional behavior and conflict. And by taking care of yourself. Beyond that...it is up to them to want it, to work a program, and to recover.

Hopeful 3 C's

While deep in crisis with my loved one, I was taught that I was powerless over the disease and didn't **Cause** it, couldn't **Control** or **Cure** it. But I *could* **Cope**, **Contribute** (in good *and* bad ways), and I can **Create** loving, healthy dialogue.

Hopeful 3 C's.

We can **Cope** in prayer, meditation, support groups, therapy, and all sorts of stress-relieving methods.

We can **Contribute** by not participating in negative behavior or conflict.

And finally...

We can **Create** healthy dialogue by keeping the bridge of communication open. We can reach out as often as we feel comfortable to remind our loved one that they are loved and we're in their corner, rooting for them to join the fight for a better life. Keep a list of available detox and treatment centers on hand for their moments of clarity, which are quick, subtle, and pass without notice sometimes (when they will say things like "You think I *want* to live like this?" or make statements related to being miserable and remembering or wanting a better life). In those moments, give those names and numbers—it's a soft, effective intervention.

Handling it that way gives us hopeful action to take without trying to control or force anything, all the while caring for yourself, keeping a safe support system on hand, and always praying, hoping and believing for the best outcome.

Like every parent, I LOVE and cherish my son. I want him happy, healthy and to grow OLD! But I am not the Author, Creator or Controller of life. We are not the Higher Power or Savior of the situation by any means. Nor do we get to call the shots when it comes to how it unfolds. Our loved one's life and recovery may not play out like we expect. In fact, most of life doesn't go according to our exact plans! There is so much peace in accepting that. That is where we remember to let faith take over versus fear. With fear calling the shots we don't make good decisions.

At one time, I thought the happy ending of our story was that "Elliot's Mom" took a strong, healthy, non-enabling, *right* approach to his addiction, thus *causing* him to get sober and create a great life! Now I know nothing could be further from the truth. There is not an ending to the story as of yet. And one thing is certain, even our "healthy" tactics can't save someone in the throes of addiction. Our best ideas for controlling or changing them are nothing more than enmeshment and over-participation. I may have helped direct him toward sobriety, but I had no power over it otherwise. The relapse part of our story puts to rest the idea that blame or heroic rescue have any control over a loved one's painful addiction. We can do every possible textbook thing and beyond, yet still not be able to cause, control, or cure anyone's way left or right.

However, the stronger and healthier we become, the better chance our loved ones and our circumstances have of becoming healthy. It's possible. A whole family can recover.

Non Deficere!

(Never give up!)

Chapter 14

Getting Through the Holiday Season with an Absent Child

During the wilderness years of family estrangement and crisis, beginning mid-October a holiday dread would begin threatening my soul like a shadow lurking around corners. I knew the holidays were coming—who didn't? We see the signs everywhere, from the grocery stores to social media: pictures of ugly sweaters and perfect family celebrations. Radio stations change format to holiday themes, shopping ads, and Christmas music. As for me, depending both upon the condition of my relationship with my son and how many miles were physically between us, I would begin measuring how much gloom I could expect to wrestle from Halloween to February.

For a parent far from their child, those weeks can feel like intense, lonely drudgery.

Unfortunately, as has been the fate of so many others, my son developed an addiction to opiate pain medication after a football injury in his teen years, and our lives have never been the same. Neither have the holidays or birthday celebrations. Through the worst of holiday seasons, I have found myself literally forcing a smile as people joyfully wished me season's greetings in passing. Meanwhile, my heart weighed a thousand pounds and my mind was a million miles away.

Familiar smells of cinnamon, apple, and pine were

reminders of the holidays long ago when we looked forward to every light, ornament, favorite Christmas show on TV, and special holiday dinner. For a few years those warm traditions have been replaced with Skype and Facetime calls.

If a family relationship was strained due to conflict caused by dysfunctional circumstances, I would instead brace myself for silence and sadness.

It took a while to force myself to believe the most tender, magical of years were behind us.

Could it really be that I would never again bundle up and walk the streets with a pack of kids in Halloween costume 'trick or treating'?

Would I really spend another Thanksgiving not having my son with me to make knowing eye-contact with when familiar family oddities played out in front of us? We call it "Eye-lish." It's our secret eye contact language when things are awkward, weird, or funny. We can communicate a whole conversation with just a glance. One look could say anything from *'Let's go!'* to *'How cute is our new nephew!'* to *'This turkey is raw'* as well as *'Can you believe she just said that? How rude!'*

Would I really never again wake up Christmas morning to my young son running in to wake me in pajamas, excited to see what gifts were waiting for him in the glow of Christmas tree lights?

My birthday is in November and his is in January. Those are days we always looked forward to making fun and special, therefore the twelve weeks from Halloween to February can sometimes pack a whole lot of gut punch.

It can be tempting to hibernate right through the festive months when everyone seems so happy and just wake up in February.

As time passes and the role of a parent changes, we might find ourselves wondering how it could be that we would have to replay these moments as memories instead of experiencing them again? Sometimes reliving the memories so many times in your mind, like movies playing on loop, you worry you'll lose them or they'll fade forever.

Sometimes moments and voices seem distant and blurry, as though they never happened. The mind can play tricks on a mother missing a child and your heart can hallucinate.

'Tis the season.

I missed my son not just as my energetic, excited child but also as I would miss a long lost friend. Our mother/son relationship didn't trespass appropriate authority—we were never best friends as peers would be. I knew I had a job to do and a responsible role to fill as a parent. But we *were friends*. Always. Our bond and connection especially through humor, or how we both always *get it* with one another in relation to life, family, and experiencing people, is something I have had with no one else quite like I have with my son, my only child.

Missing an absent son or daughter makes you marvel over how another year could possibly have swung around so fast to find you again without their presence. The jolt of being slammed with the reality of holidays *again* being so far from what we hoped they'd be is a misery I know I am not alone in experiencing.

William Shakespeare said *"Expectation is the root of all heartache,"* and I would have to agree. The heart often throbs with the disappointment of holiday expectations.

So how do you move along with the season without moping through the days like it's raining only on you?

First decide to *find* a positive outlook. Intentionally decide to find a way to see around corners and know that not every year is depressing, just as not every year is magical. Whether good or bad, no moment lasts forever. Such is life. As hard as the reality of loneliness and disappointment hits, the return of spring and future joys around the corner are just as promising.

Stoke the fire of motivation within by accepting a few fundamental truths.

First of all, you are not the only person to mournfully endure a lonely, depressing holiday season.

Many people experience great grief, loss, and pain through the holidays. Knowing you are not alone makes it easier to reject a "poor me, it's just me against the whole happy world" mentality. Recovery support groups are extremely helpful with this. Sharing stories is a great reminder that this life is give and take, someone always has it worse or better, or maybe they went through a similar struggle, came out stronger, and can speak encouragement right to your heart about it. We are able to do the same for others when it comes to adversities we've come through.

I've lived long enough to know there have been both painful years as well as years that exceed joyful expectation. This is the ebb and flow, the yin and yang of *life,* as much as the rising and setting of the sun and all four seasons are an expected part of it.

Second, know that we can sit down in the drudgery long enough to push through it.

Facing and feeling the misery like a wave crashing yet eventually subsiding is much healthier than resisting, numbing, or acting out because of it. Sometimes we need to sit in that silence and grieve our way through those moments *with* the memories. We may even fall asleep in it because an impromptu nap in a moment of meltdown always seems to help. You often wake up twenty minutes later a little less dreary, feeling stronger, more hopeful, ready to get up and proceed through that day. No matter where it falls in the calendar, we only have to get through *that* day. And if we look hard enough, we can find a lot of special moments and joy along the way.

During the coldest winters and darkest of times, we can always find ourselves buoyed along by the kindness of strangers. If we open our eyes to it, we find kindnesses around us daily. At first this can feel like trying to plant flowers in ground that is frozen solid. It's work to be hopeful and positive. It's *work* to not give up! But it's by far some of the greatest, most crucial work we'll do.

Third and finally, I believe that turning your misery and energy outward into kindhearted service is a no-fail guarantee to take you outside your world of personal circumstances.

There is nothing more uplifting than focusing on someone else for a while. There will always be someone who can use some loving kindness, whether it's a card dropped in the mail, a call to say "I was just thinking of you," or a visit to let someone else know their life matters and you want them to tell you all about it. Sometimes all one needs is a comforting reminder that they, too, are not the only one. These are things we can do to not only get by, but to give a boost to others as well. We are, in fact, all in this life together.

101

No, Halloween wasn't what it used to be the past few years. But the day was often exactly what it should have been: a beautiful Fall day with plenty of moments to appreciate and enjoy.

And yes, Thanksgiving is sometimes void of a loved one's presence. But it's still possible to spend time with family, friends, and much laughter.

The holidays are always going to come back around; we can decide make the very best of them. Having great hope that next year we will all be in a different place, and we always are. This is true about every year. Life ebbs and life flows, the sun rises and sets. In that, there is hope, as well as the reminder to stay mindful in the moment and cherish every good day without letting it slip by unnoticed.

Let's refuse to have an attitude of *'wake me up when December ends'* or *'fast forward to February!'* And instead stubbornly look for and find the kindness and joy within each day while planning for the future with a childlike hope. This awareness and hope feel more like being alive and holding the magic of the season than just about anything.

"Hope is being able to see that there is light despite the darkness." ~ Desmond Tutu

Until next year, season's greetings of hope, joy, and gratitude!

Chapter 15

Don't Tell Me to Detach

Please don't casually tell someone to *just detach* from a person they love who is actively gripped in addiction. Seriously. Please. Especially as crisis is hitting. They are probably raw and emotions are most likely raging.

There is a hopeless, sinking feeling that comes with well meaning, yet unsolicited advice when you have a loved one on a roller coaster with addiction. Often suggestions such as "Let them hit rock bottom" and "Don't enable, give tough love, just put him/her out" are so much easier said than done.

These comments only add weight to a heart already heavy with bewilderment and grief.

As a nation, we are in the midst of an addiction crisis that is not stopping. It's not even slowing down. At this point, we all know someone caught in the grip of a battle with opiates, heroin, other substances, or alcoholism. Or, at the very least we know *someone* who knows (and loves) someone who is battling. No one is exempt. It's become clear that we need a new way to view and respond to those who are struggling.

So, what do you say to someone in this storm who has deep love and concern for an addicted son or daughter, mother, brother, girlfriend, spouse...etc.? Well first of all, be mindful to tread lightly. This is an area of pain so deep and frightening, you can't imagine the added suffering careless words might cause. So tread *lightly.*

If you are the bystander watching this brutal disease from the front row, what do you do? Detach from someone you love **as** they are spiraling? What does it look like to detach? How do you abruptly cut them off?

We always hear *"you have to detach,"* but what does it actually mean?

Robert Meyers, Ph.D, from the University of New Mexico and centers for motivation and change, along with Dr. Dominique Simon-Levine, founder of AlliesInRecovery.net, have taught me a whole new way of looking at detaching, using an approach called the CRAFT method.

CRAFT is a stance, a skill set for the family. It was designed to help loved ones struggling with addiction who are resistant to stopping or getting treatment help. CRAFT is based on the knowledge that family members can play a powerful role in helping to engage the loved one who is in denial to submit to treatment. CRAFT teaches families how to communicate effectively and how to behave around someone who is actively using drugs or alcohol. Learning these skills not only encourages 70% of loved ones to enter treatment but helps a family member to lower depression, anger, and anxiety around the situation. It cleans up the mixed messages, the anger, and the frustration by using positive reinforcement, and steers clear of harsh, potentially explosive confrontation. Family members know their loved one best. In addition to learning how to intervene, by applying the skills of CRAFT, families also decrease the conflict in the relationship and help guide the loved one toward recovery.

Those who are actively addicted usually came to this condition one of two ways: due to a medical need after an injury, or because they were seeking the hope produced by connection to someone or something. Therefore, how disconnected might they already feel? Being cut off from love and support when they are in dire need of it is no solution.

Cutting off those we love only adds to everyone's misery and shame.

What if instead of detaching we were to...*attach?* Attach kindness, love, comfort, positive reinforcement? To someone who has become untrustworthy? Who has brought chaos, upset and drama into our lives? How? That is counter to the advice most of us have received.

The common misconception is that attaching puts us passively in the line of fire. That is not my take at all. We don't have to pay off anyone's debts or clean up their consequences. But instead of tough love, we can learn to give *smart* love. Our boundaries must change according to the circumstances— different access to the home, our time, our resources, etc. Yet, there is still a strong show of love, support, and concern.

When we were in our hurricane season of opiate dependency and my son needed to recover, all I ever heard were things like the tough love, rock bottom, detachment advice. With a broken heart full of fear and sorrow, I attempted to try these suggestions. The truth is, I *couldn't* bring myself to cut him off completely. There were even times I hid conversations with my son from those around me who'd exasperatedly advised me to go silent toward him. I wasn't withholding the information because I felt it was wrong to call him and tell him I loved him dearly and would always wait for him to want better. I held back because I didn't want to face *their* disapproval. My contact with him would mean I was "doing it wrong" in their eyes.

Ugh. What *garbage* that was! Even if it was well-meaning. How could a person who hadn't been down this road possibly know what I should be doing? We were all winging it based on knowledge stemming mostly from reruns of the sensationalized TV show Intervention. Nothing I was doing (or *not* doing) was working and harsh tactics were only driving a painful wedge tightly between my son and me.

As Dr. Simon-Levine mentions often in her teachings, rather than methods of "surprise party interventions" where loved ones are deceived into a gathering, group-shamed about their life, and given ultimatums. With CRAFT, a softer, less-threatening approach is recommended. A better way of asking a loved one to please go into treatment would be in a safe, loving environment. Such as two people sitting across a table from one another over breakfast. With kindness and compassion, yet firmly outlining expectations and suggestions. With numbers in hand of treatment center options.

Detaching from the chaos, conflict, and consequences your loved one may reap is one thing. Detaching from the *person*, to the point of no contact, is another. We can have our addicted loved ones present in our lives with safeguards and limits in place. *Things will move at the speed of trust.* We can reach out as often as we want to let them know they are precious to us while choosing not to be around the chaos, conflict, or consequences of the disease.

We need each other. Disconnecting is misery. Connecting is helpful and healing even if that's not immediately seen. And in that there is relief and great hope.

I am personally some years past the most traumatic of those days. Even still, I am more than glad I never told my son when his life was at its most desperate,

"You can't call me, you won't hear from me, you won't have your *mom* in your life."

As bad as our disputes were, as much as I cut off access to comforts, I could not, *I would not* cut him off from *me*. And I never will.

If that is viewed as wrong, I really don't need to be right.

Chapter 16

Showing up on Someone's Hard Day

There's a lot to be said for someone who shows up and sits by your side in the midst of a *hard,* hard time. Whether it's after an unusually bad day, on the heels of tragic news, in a moment of stress from a job loss, in the presence of your fears and worries for your child, or any of the complex discouragements that occur along the roads of life. It's a special kind of person that will show up as a *presence* in your midst when you are in suffering, heartache, or despair.

There were times when my family was in crisis and I felt lost and alone in our tragic situation, going through what felt like unending heartache. Emotions could surge out of control—it felt like my heart was hemorrhaging. It was hard to breathe in public.

As many do, I endured it alone for months, isolating, tucking my head and braving my way through. But the strain finally became unbearable to handle alone. I reached out by email to a handful of trusted family and friends and simply said "This is harder than I've let on and I'm overwhelmed. Please come by if you can."

And so they came.

Within hours one after another they came. First was a family friend who came to the door straight from a yoga session to sit with me. "Let's look at one aspect at a time," he suggested. "I'm going to think about all you are bearing as if it were happening to me. What would I do? What *have* I done? Let's triage it together. *You're not alone.*" He left me with more hope that day that I'd had in a long time. My soul felt strengthened. I was greatly encouraged and inspired just from his presence.

Next was my sister. She skipped an important class and drove over an hour to get to me. She sat quiet in the presence of my tears, as my worries and fears spilled out. Thing after thing after detail after thing I felt hurt by, worried about, and so on. "We're in this together, *you are not alone.*" she said, leaving me with a couple of solutions to consider.

A couple of hours later another friend called and said "I want you to know you can go to bed tonight knowing I'm here, you have options, you've got a friend in me. I'll show up in a moment if you need me, just call. *You don't have to go through it alone.*" Tears of relief silently rolled from my eyes as I whispered "Thank you, you have no idea what a comfort that is."

Something about the presence of humanity in the midst of heartache breathes life into a drowning soul, even before solutions appear. Comfort, presence, and kindness versus a lecture, advice, or any identifying of where I might've gone wrong. No cliché, or empty "chin up, hang in there" type sentiments. When we are met with the opposite, the power of "We're in this *together*" somehow allows healing to begin.

Sometimes all we need is a moment of compassion. In the presence of kindness, we are encouraged enough to get up and face our way through another day.

It's important to be mindful and aware as a soul traveling this life's experience. Being present in the right now so that you can face life with peace is, I believe, the way to enlightenment and joy. But to show up and be present in someone *else's* moment is indeed a powerful thing. Having experienced the healing power that human kindness offers, I so encourage it. If anyone you know is suffering from loneliness, heartache, bad news, or going through a downtrodden time, consider showing up and being present with them. Call, text, drop a note in the mail, go to the door to say "I don't know what's going to happen, I don't know what got you to this point or what's going to get you through it; I just want you to know *you're not alone in this.*"

You could make the difference between strength and hope, rather than tears and despair.

And for those suffering the weight of a burden alone, it's okay to reach out and ask for help and comfort. You will be amazed at the level of kindness others are able to extend. We are, after all, in this life together.

Chapter 17

Trigger Happy: When I Feel Triggered

What does it mean to be *"triggered?"*

For me, being triggered means something (or *someone*) has hit a nerve. An emotional bruise has been poked, exposing infection. In some way a "button has been pushed." We can then feel launched into upset, stress, grief, anger, road rage, fear, insecurity, jealousy, etc.

Extreme triggers cause fight, flight, or freeze and some ignite recurring symptoms of PTSD.

In the days before I aggressively did the work to calm my life, being triggered could result in a distressed mood that might last hours and even days. If poked hard enough, I could be triggered into despair, worry, bewilderment, and isolation.

I no longer allow people or circumstances to take the reins emotionally, but it was a struggle for years, particularly when life included crisis.

I know that I am not alone. One day I took to the public to ask:

What do you do when you're triggered?

The answers were quite varied and included the following:

Eat, watch TV, write songs, play guitar, or listen to music.

I tend to want a drink.

Go quiet, internalize my feelings until the burn is gone. Call and confide in someone trustworthy.

One person elaborated and said, *"I'm at a point in my life where I know it's best not to react, but my ego initially doesn't want me to turn the other cheek. So I will plot all kinds of juicy, painful, brutal revenge. Then in an hour or so I remember I am supposed to be an adult and I always let it go. I believe we reap what we sow and I never want to be on the hook for some childish revenge."*

One man told me, *"I find a distraction, call and bullsh*t with a friend, or listen to music."*

One mom said, *"I eat lots of sweets! My daughter's addiction caused me to pack on 20 extra pounds!"*

* * *

A therapist described a habit to me that he turns to in moments of emotional triggering. He will often respond by ordering from an online shopping site and tracking his purchase. Every few hours he logs into the site and checks the status. The day his purchase is due to arrive, he checks every few minutes. He said he will become so engrossed in the process that he will leave work and rush home between appointments to see if he can time his car to meet the delivery truck in the drive way!

Although he will engage in the habit for a few days, he realizes he is doing this in order to avoid some uncomfortable feeling. Perhaps he was needing to have a conversation with a colleague that might get heavy and is dreading it. "Ahhh, *now* would be the perfect time to order a new book about therapy!" he thinks out loud.

"It really doesn't matter what's causing my discomfort—this is almost always my go to response" he told me, "Even though I am a therapist, like anyone I can get triggered. I have to remind even myself what's healthiest is to stop and just *be* with whatever I'm feeling."

Being triggered tends to kick us into procrastination and distractions.

When painfully triggered, I used to do all of that and then some. There were times, for example, when I found myself triggered or dreading something difficult and before facing it, I would instead scroll mindlessly through social media. I would almost always eventually come across something that made me feel irritated, sorry for myself, insecure, frustrated, or negative in some way. This added to the gloom I was already wallowing in.

These days, mindfulness and wisdom usually prevail. Now if something causes my heart to drop or heat to rise within me, I pull away for a few minutes to breathe or walk my dog, usually recapping things I am grateful for in order from A to Z. That never fails to calm and reroute my thoughts.

I also suggest applying the "90-second rule" when a nerve has been struck. Meaning, pull away from whatever is triggering for a 90-second break. Stepping away to refocus puts us in a different chemical and emotional space.

We are then much more clear and better able to deal with the issue at hand. Or maybe, *not* deal. If it's something that doesn't deserve your response, taking a break can give clarity enough to not engage hostile situations that are best left to themselves.

One thing we can count on in life is this: triggers will always present themselves. Having a planned response will minimize regret over mishandling them.

Suggested responses for when triggers occur:

Deep breathing: take a step back in the midst of the situation and inhale a four-count breath, hold it for two counts and exhale it for four counts. Do this five or six times. This breathing technique floods peace and oxygen to the extremities and sets us on neutral just long enough that we don't easily rush into madness with anyone. If I'm still surging with adrenaline, I will do it again or take a walk alone before allowing myself to react or make any decisions.

Get moving: having a normal exercise schedule has many benefits. Also helpful in the moment when triggered find a hallway or a room where you can go alone for a minute or two and do 10-20 jumping jacks to boost positive energy.

Five senses: Look around you and identify **five** things you can see, **four** things you can touch, **three** things you can hear, **two** things you can smell, and **one** thing you can taste.

Write it down, rip it up: when you are able, write down what you are feeling and why, what you feel like doing, what you hope happens (even if it's evil in the moment, evil thoughts do not make you evil, acting on them is what gets us in trouble!) and then dispose of what you wrote.

A moment of gratitude: stop to remind yourself of three things you are grateful for. Gratitude shifts energy

Lift someone's spirits: give a sincere compliment via card, call, email, or text to someone who might need some kind, uplifting words.

Again, triggers will always present themselves. It even happens to therapists. Instead of running with them, I now acknowledge them. "Oh, hi trigger, it's you again. Let me get myself to get to a calm, peaceful place before I respond."

Applying that in the moment is the key. It's a process. Growth is always painful at first, but the acquired strength, peace, and serenity is well worth the effort.

Recovery efforts work! These days my triggers, are like annoying flies, whereas before they were like elephants.

"And the day came when the risk it took to remain tight in the bud was more painful than the risk it took to bloom." ~ Anonymous

Chapter 18

A House Divided Stands No Chance

Divorce, Division and the Disease of Addiction

I think any respectful, right-minded person would agree that it's important within a group or family setting to be on the same page when making decisions and navigating circumstances. This is especially true as it relates to managing crisis.

While we all may agree that unity is critical, this ideal is useless if our actions don't corroborate our claims. We can all find ourselves locking horns with those we're called to unite with for a common cause.

When the goal is centered around a loved one who struggles with substances, *united not divided* is of utmost importance.

If division is occurring within the home (or homes), it's crucial to resolve differences in a fair and honest manner in order to obtain peaceful solutions.

Concerning alcoholism, addiction, and SUD, most people have stories of division. Some occur within a marriage where everyone in the household is pulled in different directions. There can be a good cop/bad cop situation in play, siblings played against one another, and so on.

Coming to terms with the huge importance of having a united front is crucial.

In families where there has been a divorce, it would

seem division may be already in place, but from my own experience I know that unity is possible.

Division may come from well-intended family members or friends. Division can come from people pulled in or perhaps outsiders taking it upon themselves to become involved. Division can be motivated by fear, guilt, or more sinister motives such as selfishness or a hidden agenda. Whatever the case may be, division is an area of weakness that allows the disease of addiction and the manipulation it needs to survive, to wreak absolute havoc within a family.

Cracks of division, similar to cracks in a foundation, will bring a house down. Wherever those cracks appear, deception and manipulation can get in, which will deter truth and peace and can postpone the path to recovery.

My personal experience

I don't write as an expert; I write from experience. The following is my experience with solutions in place for division:

- *Divorced not Divided*

My ex-husband and I kept a pretty good truce going for the decade we shared the responsibility of raising our son after our divorce. Of course it was awkward and even hostile in the initial phases of separating. In the early days we were prone to heated conversations and blame (never in the presence of our son) and it made for discomfort when our paths crossed.

Two years after the divorce, we met in person to have a conversation that cleared the air, we put our issues to rest, and moved forward with a commitment to positively parent our child. We set clear guidelines to return to prevent our exchanges from becoming cluttered with issues.

This allowed for strong unity when SUD and crisis came roaring through our lives later.

The following are a few ways we avoided division going forward:

Decide on goals and ground rules

Goals:

Have common goals: peace, health, happiness, and well-being for every child you share is of the highest priority. Never forget, it's about *them*.

Giving our shared child a fighting chance at the life of stability we felt we didn't get growing up was important. Giving our son a strong sense of family despite having divorced parents was crucial. These goals were important as a lifestyle for the years prior to crisis, and they became priority during.

Ground Rules:

Anything you do or say (within reason) ***won't be held against you.*** We can choose to not have paper thin skin in dealing with one another. Cooler heads must prevail. If you make a mistake you are still respected as an important part of the family. It's not going to get rubbed in your face. Moving on is constant.

Let's not demonize one another. It is never healthy to say negative or destructive things about someone your child half-identifies with. If a child is not under threat of serious harm, truths will come out if they need to. Attacking one another and shoving poison in the ear of your shared child(ren) causes confusion, negativity, and will pave the way for unneeded struggles for *them* down the road.

Let's not rush to react, pounce on, or punish each other. Not everything is an ordeal to freak out about. Making a mistake does not classify you as the villain of our equation.

I prioritized this, having come from a condemning, shaming, punishing background. Which is a very difficult culture to be a part of—it makes it impossible to relax enough to just *be*. If one lays in wait for another to mess up in order to pounce, there can never truly be peace.

No petty, spiteful moves. That would only be wounds from the past manipulating current behavior. This includes not planting negative seeds about one another in the mind of a child. No competitive parenting, such as good guy versus bad guy mentalities. If one needs to lose for the other to win, not only does no one really win, but the shared child, group, and goals are the real losers.

Incidentally, it's good to remember that the behavior we engage in may turn up later in our sons and daughters. If I am engaging in (or accommodating) spiteful, manipulative, game-playing, unfair tactics, chances are my son will grow up to date, marry, or become someone like that. By virtue of this behavior being woven as if normal into the fabric of his being, he may come to believe it's acceptable and okay. It's not acceptable or okay.

Those things will always come back to bite.

Agree to approach things humbly and bypass childishness. Our sons and daughters are way too important for us to engage in arrogant, right-fighting immaturity. It really helps to be a proud "I *don't* know-it-all." It's not about just one of us, our history, our unresolved feelings, or who is the better parent. *It's about the goal: the well-being of our kid(s).* We must compromise, come to agreement as much as possible and unite for what is right, fair, and true. This is about what is best for the greater good.

White flags go up immediately. When it comes to our sons and daughters, cease-fire should be quick, regardless of how we may feel about one another. If we are at odds, a peace treaty can still happen by virtue of having a shared mission.

Many times in our situation we could be aggravated with one another or at odds, yet still always have the safety and ability to call and say "I have to tell you what just happened."

Loyalty to the goal, to the truth and to what is fair and right. We don't need to fight just to win. Logic overrules emotion.

These standards greatly mattered to us when our son was young, they later became the strength from which we navigated him to a healthy place when our lives were in crisis.

* * *

What do the earlier years have to do with the disease of addiction? Plenty—addiction is a family disease. If the time ever comes when we might deal with issues of addiction within the family, we have a great running start against the behaviors fueled by SUD. With goals in place, we have strategies ready for managing crisis, manipulation, and division in the future.

And that can prove to be life (and sanity) saving.

Will we ever fail when it comes to abiding by the ground rules? Absolutely. Sometimes miserably! We don't always get it right. But the foundation laid is always there to return to no matter who drops the ball. You live, you learn, you do the next right thing and keep going.

* * *

What if it's not possible to agree and unite or if

the efforts are one-sided?

Understandably, there are people we all have to deal with that refuse to play by the rules. Some operate with low-blow behavior, don't care for the greater good, and can't be trusted to be sincere. Other times, too much damage has been done to have safe, vulnerable communication. There are people not motivated by logic, fairness, or peace. Some folks prefer to keep the fires of conflict and discord burning.

In these situations, the reality is they are probably not going to change behaviors or become less difficult. However, we can set good boundaries and remain healthy enough within ourselves that our reactivity is not negative alongside them.

Personally, in those cases I believe it's a thing of honor to choose to be the one who still does what is right, staying committed to integrity, boundaries and decisions, holding hope for a peaceful outcome, despite anyone else's decisions. Their journey is theirs to figure out—we are responsible for our own.

Show kindness, don't ever interact with vitriol, respond with dignity, and keep moving forward.

* * *

Nelson Mandela lived by the "Ubuntu" principle. The concept is, "I need you in order to be me; and you need me in order to be you."

We need each other. We need to be kind and respectful with one another because we **need** each other.

I am thankful my ex-husband and I were able to establish unity when there was so much opportunity for division. It's possible if we all do our part.

Our mission is to give our sons and daughters a strong family which in turn will give them a fighting chance for a healthy adult life.

Our responsibility *is to not further discord, conflict, or chaos.*

Our outcome *can be the creation of a unique family unit that will become a safe haven, which in turn makes it easier for our sons and daughters to choose a healthy adult life in which they can thrive.*

My story *is not a beautifully packaged family tale. It is raw and real. But it is a true story of reality, recovery, hard work and hope.*

Peace is possible!

Chapter 19

Silver Linings

Can good come out of terrible crisis and despair? How can we possibly find a silver lining when it comes to a son or daughter (or any loved one) struggling with alcoholism or addiction?

While I would wish a loved one struggling with substance use disorder (SUD) on *no* family, I do believe when facing this affliction, strengths do emerge out of the depths of despair. Adversities also cause a purge of what's unnecessary and toxic from our lives.

I can say in my own life positives did manifest after the tornado of addiction swept through our home. Let me first explain that I am in no way saying it's a lighthearted thing for a family to face the horrors of addiction. What I am saying is that there are silver linings in terrible circumstances. At least there have been for us. When it comes to the dark cloud of despair that completely changed the trajectory of our lives, some good emerged after the storm.

To name a few...

Recovery

When my son left the state to pursue recovery, health, and wellness, we weren't sure what direction our lives would take. We were all pretty much shell shocked. No change that starts with upheaval seems positive in the beginning.

But now, more than five years later, here we are with so many unexpected gifts and blessings in place, it's hard to believe we're the same people.

One of those gifts is the lifestyle of recovery.

It was at a young age of adulthood when my son began working a recovery program. Meaning he regularly meets with others to discuss life experiences, struggles, strengths, and triumphs in order to make progress and maintain healthy accountability.

I joined the program myself two years later.

Thinking back to that age, I would say working on self-awareness, rigorous honesty, and emotional health were not the course of study for most of us. What a gift to address these vital areas at such an early stage of life!

There's only so much as parents we can do to prepare our children for adulthood. Eventually it's up to them to make their own choices and flesh them out. And then live with, and learn from the results.

It takes every moment, every twist and turn in our children's lives to mold them into strong, independent, capable men and women. We can't control or predict what path might be necessary for them to become respectable, capable, strong adults. At some point we have to let them go, remind them of all they've been taught, watch them rise and sometimes see them fall. It's all part of the journey.

"Few things help an individual more than to place responsibility upon him and let him know that you trust him." ~ Booker T. Washington, The Booker T. Washington Society

* * *

Removal

By sheer virtue of how urgent our situation was, my life went through a major detox in the midst of those years. It was as if a great purge took place. Over time, due to recovery work and regular therapy, I found I was working my way out of toxic thinking that led to equally toxic situations and relationships. And I had many.

Truthfully, most of my connections with people were in one way or another out of balance, unfair, unhealthy, or negative. We can spend years not realizing this. It was a necessary time of cleansing. What we lose or let go of in a storm often ends up being for the best.

When you are struggling to manage your household and grasp sanity in the midst of circumstances that are life and death, you have no time to play games or navigate frustrating, high-maintenance involvements.

Those things truly just don't matter.

A family member in active addiction is at times as urgent as being in a house rapidly filling with fire. When that's the case, you will gather only the things that are most important and let go of what might weigh you down.

We are all on different journeys and sometimes a connection, like a shoe, just doesn't fit. It's not meant to go the distance with us. That's perfectly okay. Wish them well and keep moving.

* * *

Renovation

As a family, working your way out of conflict, misery, and fear is the largest part of the recovery process. In fact, those things are often resident within you for decades, until crisis hits and exposes what you're made of and have been carrying inside. When we come face to face with ourselves, if we truly dig in and do the work to recover, we can free ourselves from life-*long* areas of struggle.

For example, the grief and anger from the wounded child I continued to identify with as an adult always remained with me. Misery and worthlessness were a profound part of the fabric of who I was—they whispered to me relentlessly. When you hit a threshold of suffering in the midst of circumstances, you can break free all of that.

Purging internal miseries is a profound silver lining. The impact of harboring terror for your child's life pretty well demolishes anything unnecessary in our lives that needs to go. We come out of those years a completely different person. It's not possible to remain the same after a life-and-death scare with a son or daughter.

I came out of those years a million times braver and stronger.

"Something is going to come out of this. Something new. This can end you up in a whole new place – a better place, a much more open place." ~Pema Chodron

* * *

Reward

While much was removed from my life, many great things were added. As a result of what was at one time terrible, I found my way into "the rooms." You will meet some of the finest people in the programs of Nar-Anon, Al-Anon, and many other support group rooms. They become family (except maybe not as dysfunctional!).

Our struggles also reward us with a powerful awakening in relationships that survive the trauma.

We can see a dramatic deepening of love, friendship, compassion, and value for the relationships that survived our storm. A new level of gratitude is born.

Another silver lining is the courage to pursue new and lofty goals. After my own life was literally gutted by crisis, I found a new level of confidence. You develop the boldness to go for things you probably didn't have had the courage to even consider before.

Strength developed in the struggle pushes us to new levels of fearlessness and motivation.

* * *

A Call to Rally

I believe the raging opiate epidemic in this country is a mass call to action. It's not stopping—it's not even slowing down. The horror of it is forcing people to open their eyes, face truths, and hopefully pursue information, help, and healthy decisions.

There is nothing good about an epidemic of addiction plaguing communities, ripping apart families, and taking lives. But one silver lining is that society as a whole is being called to roll up our sleeves, look at our lives, make different choices, and extend compassion.

Light can be found even in the presence of deep darkness.

Our lives have all completely changed. How could they not? In many ways they changed for the better. We were literally shaken awake to the two things that matter the most in this life—people and time.

It should never get lost on us that hardship and crisis of *any* sort may fall upon our lives, no one can predict what might happen, and no one is immune. Life can drop you to your knees in a moment. But the silver lining is, once we've weathered the storms, we are better equipped to handle them in the future. Beyond that, in the calm, we become powerfully aware of the value of today.

"Birds sing after a storm; why shouldn't people feel as free to delight in whatever remains to them?" ~Rose F. Kennedy

Chapter 20

Disappointment and Grief: Finding a New Normal

When it comes to dealing with addiction and family dysfunction, two adjacent visitors are disappointment and grief. Which for me, are interwoven. Grief involves loss, which means hopes deflate into disappointment, as plans and visions for life are redirected, if not completely cut off.

I'm very familiar with the shock of upheaval and change, along with the processes of struggle and resistance that soon follow. Many times I've had to make my way through dark times to reach a place of acceptance before I could find peace and hope.

In my own life, I have personally experienced three significant seasons of loss, grief, and disappointment. As a result of those times, I've grieved the loss of people, homes, pets, and plans.

The first experience was during the death of my father which mercilessly occurred during my divorce. The second was after my son experienced an injury in football and a dependency on pain medication resulted, tearing through our lives like an out of control freight train.

The third was when my son moved out of state, just before the sudden death of our dog that we loved like crazy, as a handful of other unexpected things happened and turned life upside down. Without warning, I found myself becoming an empty nester almost overnight, with more than a few heart-wrenching circumstances to sort my way through. I was in deep grief, mourning the life I thought we would have. It was a lot to process.

Loss. Shock. Change. Upheaval.

I don't know about you, but for me—when it rains it pours.

In these times we become wide awake and acutely aware of our lives. All senses are heightened. Seeming to emotionally and even physically lose balance, every familiar frame of reference feels altered. As we trudge through our worst days it can be hard to breathe through our circumstances.

(Please note—if you're close to someone with a loved one is struggling with addiction, or other types of loss, shock, change or upheaval, it's a powerful thing to come alongside with comfort and presence. Gestures of kindness and compassion are *extremely* potent boosts of encouragement and hope for anyone enduring dark, painful days.)

* * *

Finding a new normal

Finding hope again takes time. It's a process and we may experience a few of the five stages of grief (denial, anger, bargaining, depression, and acceptance) before reconciling ourselves to how different life is actually panning out from what we'd envisioned.

After loss, change, and disappointment, things will never be the same, but that doesn't mean life can't become good again.

Sometimes things fall apart and are rebuilt stronger, and better. There are times when a massive life change is actually an awakening to the value of life.

I once had an awe inspiring conversation in passing with an older man named Brad. After commenting about his noticeable energy and enthusiasm, Brad began explaining how he developed his zest for life. He told me he went through a heartbreaking divorce years prior, one he didn't expect or want. He was beyond devastated and quite naturally uncertain how to face starting over again in life. Brad described for me how it seemed as though one day he was grilling dinner in his backyard, mowing the lawn, driving a sedan, and planning to spend the rest of his days doing so...to the next, sitting alone in a one room apartment in the city, isolated and bewildered. His life had become unrecognizable.

I believe many of us who have suffered loss and upheaval can relate.

The defeat and loss he felt were overwhelming, lasting months and months. One day, a friend concerned with his dismal outlook stopped by to see Brad. Immediately, this friend took it upon himself to schedule a fishing trip to Miami where for the next few days he spoke hope and possibility back into Brad's despairing soul.

Stepping outside of his routine of loss and hopelessness woke Brad up to the idea of a new lease on life.

When Brad returned from the trip, he thought long and hard about his unfortunate change of circumstances. He decided to take the reins of his life without focusing on unfairness or blame. He chose to begin truly *living*.

Brad told me ever since setting his mind on living, he intentionally wakes up every morning with the motto, "What great moments can I experience today?"

He gets up at 5 a.m. five days a week to work out and meditate, spending time on his physical, spiritual, and mental health before heading to his business. Some days he does something extraordinarily thoughtful and special for someone close to him. Weekly he signs up for a workout class he would have never tried before. Just as often he will stop into a new coffee shop or boutique to try something he'd never heard of and leave a large, unexpected tip...and so on. He keeps life flowing this way, free from becoming stale, idle or stagnant.

On a daily basis, Brad runs his life at this enthusiastic pace. Once he got into the habit, it became his lifestyle, and he's lived this way for more than two decades. Listening, I couldn't help but catch his enthusiasm!

This once distraught man who thought life was over is now in his seventies and has not missed out on a single day. He's more active and alive than many who are a third his age! Brad opened my eyes to the possibility of living a life fully awake to the value of time.

What seemed at first like a ruined life ended up being a change of direction toward a life he may have missed out on had he not experienced loss and disappointment.

Not that he would have wished for divorce—does anyone? But sometimes you just have to play the hell out of the hand you're dealt.

Brad's attitude is truly an example of someone who took adversity and turned it into his motivation for making the most of all of his days.

It takes time, healing, support, and mindfulness – but life can become whole again after loss, shock, change, and upheaval. It's often after great darkness that we become most aware of the value of light.

Those who have been broken are always able to love harder than most. Once you've been in the depths of darkness, you learn to appreciate the light.

* * *

End note:

"The thing about suffering life-changing tragedy— afterwards you are profoundly unafraid. When you've faced the worst sorrow and fear life could possibly bombard you with, what worries are you left with? What can anyone do to hurt you after that? You become permanently unafraid and free of the petty concerns that tragedy-free people get caught up in. And in some small way, that's a comfort. This is a truth I've paid dearly to claim—I don't scare as easily as I used to."

I jotted this notion down at a Women's conference during author Barbara Johnson's talk. Barbara has many published books on finding one's way through the deep, horrendous waters of grief. While I personally cannot speak as someone who knows the agony of losing a child, Barbara writes with full knowledge having lost two. Her books are about finding hope and even joy again. I cannot recommend them enough for anyone struggling through the grief of unimaginable loss.

Some losses will always be with us—the loss of a child, partner, or any close, precious and much loved person. It changes the dynamics of who we are and how we live. Life becomes a matter of managing the loss while carrying their absence within us. In their honor and with the best of memories, we must continue to live and find our way forward until we meet them again.

Chapter 21

Guard Your Valuables! What We Need to Protect

Because I write openly about my struggles and recovery from trauma, I often get letters asking what I might do in certain situations involving deep, hostile family conflict or the madness that ensues from an issue of addiction or alcoholism in a home. In years past, I didn't have many "tools in the toolbox" for navigating those troubled waters. I'm certainly no expert. But I am experienced when it comes to turmoil and crisis. By the time our crisis transpired and in the moments when dormant issues exploded to the surface (as they are prone to do when left unattended), I realized I needed strategies in place for managing tough times and intense emotions when they occur.

First and foremost, having faith and gratitude can be some of the strongest power tools we possess. Combined, the two empower us to forgive, find hope, let go, make peace, adapt to extremely difficult situations, and get back up (over and over).

Beyond this, a set of "tools" to pull out on an as needed basis is vital. Those I have found useful have been...

Knowing who you are

For most of my life I allowed a background of dysfunction and the issues in my life to cause me to feel intrinsically worthless. When we come up through a toxic mess, we believe our identity to be based out of every area of deficit, which results in even more toxic connections and environments. Because it's our normal.

Like many, I personally thought I deserved less than anyone. I spent years second guessing myself and not trusting my intuition even when it shouted at me. I'd usually believe someone else had more authority to be right about me than I did. Many times after things took a wrong turn, I'd look back and see all the signs I had ignored because I simply didn't believe in myself.

When this is your thought pattern, you're at the mercy of everyone around you. You will believe that drawing lines, setting boundaries, and sticking up for yourself are selfish things. But they're not selfish, they're healthy.

Unless we know who we are and that we were *fundamentally created* with value, we become easy prey for those with a dysfunctional agenda.

Therapy and recovery work

Therapy is not for the faint of heart. Therapy and recovery are strong tools that serve to identify and separate us from our issues.

Spending time with a counselor is not a sign of weakness. It's actually quite brave to admit that we're struggling with something. (Therapy probably kept me from having a mug shot).

How much better to just be real and get it over with than to pretend we're not in a struggle, put on a mask, and end up acting it out.

Spiritual Life

Alongside therapy and recovery, great tools to rely on are regular spiritual practices. We can prop ourselves *up* on faith and find there to be no better support.

During more than a few major storms, while facing what I felt were huge obstacles and impossible odds, I discovered that I could *always* find comfort in the Higher Power of my life. The Unseen Force of kindness and strength that is always for me, always helping, healing and strengthening me. The Presence of peace that never leaves us in the worst of times. Even when it feels like everyone else has.

The reminder to: "Guard your valuables!"

This incredibly powerful tool was a piece of advice frequently given to me more than a decade ago and it took almost as long to fully grasp it.

I have a close friend who counsels families in crisis, I would sometimes call her to complain about whatever emotional injury du' jour that I'd sustained. Usually my frustration pertained to a snide comment from a friend or coworker that was delivered at the worst possible time. Or maybe it was an issue I was having with my mom, another relative, or my son.

Her response was never to shame them and baby me (which is important), but instead to point out that once again I "hadn't protected my valuables."

"You didn't guard your valuables." she would gently remind me.

"What are my valuables?" I'd asked in confusion.

"That's your problem, you don't know." she said more than a few times. "When you figure them out, you'll protect them."

We established over time that valuables are the things that make up who we *are*. Guarding our valuables involves protecting our confidence, peace of mind, goals, problems, sorrows, dreams, and opinions, the deep places of the heart.

Guarding your valuables means being cautious with who we reveal what is going on in our life.

She would also suggest that valuables are how we respond to others *and* allow them to speak to us. Self-respect and dignity are valuables.

We aren't protecting ourselves when we've felt uncomfortable or unsafe around certain people yet didn't give ourselves enough support to create a safe distance from them. We need to honor those gut feelings instead of second guessing ourselves or thinking it might be rude to be guarded.

You can only spend so many years being pulled along by others before ending up burned out and resentful, not realizing you're betraying yourself. This is how we regularly give away our power and identity. When you live like that, it will put you at the mercy of everyone around you.

The more we grow in the knowledge of our worth and rights in those areas, the healthier our mind will become and over time confidence begins to grow.

My wise friend's advice was a specific way of identifying boundaries along with methods of protecting myself within them. Life-saving.

* * *

Other valuables might include:

Who we spend time with

Who we do favors for, who we allow to vent to us, who we allow to know our confidential personal business, who knows us on intimate levels, and so on. These are valuable parts of us that we need to treasure and protect.

If we don't know that—that is where the recovery work needs to be done.

We attract the results of the work we do. If we haven't done much work on ourselves and our sense of value, we end up surrounded by people who don't think of us much either.

Rigorous Honesty

In order to recover, we have to uncover.

This is a time-saving power tool. Rigorous honesty makes life a whole lot easier when we cut to the chase. Nothing can block the flow of energy that honesty carries. **Truth** is a power tool.

Self-awareness

Recognizing your participation in an unhealthy situation is a giant step toward freedom from it.

Knowing yourself, trusting your intuition when it checks you (it will *always* check you—it's our built in safety system!) will protect you from being desperately hurt by people who pretend to be one thing and turn out to be another.

Open, honest, safe communication

Healthy people communicate; unhealthy people manipulate.

Maintaining peace and equanimity in the midst of chaos

Ignore those who always come running to you like their hair is on fire.

My favorite word is **equanimity**. Equanimity is the ability to maintain mental calmness and composure when in a difficult situation.

There are personalities who come at you to try to force

you on your heels. Some people thrive on conflict, shock value, etc. Ambushes can trigger us. We have to work to remain mindful and composed. Maintaining equanimity and enough presence of mind to not merge energy with someone else's negativity, or "hair on fire" urgency, is the goal.

Education and Information are life preserving power tools

Within my own life, I prefer to have clear understanding of what is going on and what steps I need to take to find solutions. Becoming informed and educated might mean going to the internet for information, taking my questions to professionals, calling friends with similar experiences, finding books, classes and workshops on the subject, or having a counselor or therapist to call and check in with in times of stress or confusion.

When it comes to issues of addiction, alcoholism, substance use disorder and the dysfunctional behaviors they involve, clarity is the doorway to resolution. Knowing the patterns of the brain disease of addiction, understanding the situation at hand, and having tools in place when times get desperate will help build boundaries around your peace (and sanity).

A Strong Healthy Support System

We all need someone to have our back and we need to be that for others in return. The ebb and flow of support is what heals people. I cannot stress the importance of support enough. Friends to call, a recovery group, a family support group, a *unit* that is compassionate, kind, and treats us with sincere, positive regard will heal just about anything.

* * *

Having strategies and tools on hand for tough times are as important for our lives as a toolbox or first aid kit.

When a tornado rips a house apart, once the storm is over life does go forward, yet it's different than before. We can't just proceed as usual now that the winds have stopped. There's damage to deal with and rebuilding that must take place. It takes time to gather the tools to build stronger lives. It's a process.

Speaking from personal experience, it's one that is definitely worth it.

Peace and equanimity are possible.

Chapter 22

Conflict: What Role Do You Play in the Drama Triangle?

Conflict is a part of the human experience. It can be necessary and sometimes it can be nasty.

Drama resulting from dysfunction, addiction, and alcoholism often centers around conflict. That can be some of the most stressful elements when dealing with the disorder of substance abuse.

Some months ago I learned that dysfunctional conflict often involves what has been dubbed the "Drama Triangle" by Psychiatrist Stephen Karpman. This theory implies that within conflict we each play the role of:

Victim: powerless, hopeless and stuck.

Persecutor: critical, blaming, controlling, superior.

Hero: pain reliever, rescuer, keeps victims helpless.

We revolve in and out of each one.

Do you see yourself in this?

Many times I've stood in these roles. In past disputes I tended to veer back and forth between the victim and the hero. I didn't realize how much I liked being both. But I could be a pretty good blamer too.

No matter which role, I was somehow always wronged **and** always right.

We're often hard-pressed to self-examine and

consider *our* unhealthy participation in conflict due to the effects of whoever, *whatever* is coming against us. But once we become of aware of unhealthy patterns, we can't **unknow** them. Therefore, we're not granted the luxury of resorting back to them. Those who are smart don't get to play dumb. We are no longer the victim, hero or persecutor. We're a **participant** in the cycle.

No matter how infected the situation, healthier ways of handling conflict are possible. Information on how to modify our lives around this subject is available if we're interested in improving and pursuing peaceful lives. CRAFT method and Verbal Judo are excellent tools for managing conflict and hostile situations.

* * *

We've all seen situations where those once in close relationship had a disagreement and instead of settling the matter in order to move forward, they turned adversarial. This resulted in a once resolvable conflict becoming a toxic feud.

The truth is, when it comes to conflict some people live for it and many don't fight fair.

Rebecca, a mother struggling with a daughter's substance abuse issues called me earlier this year in deep distress. Her call wasn't about her daughter this time; it was about trouble she was having with a friend she had been close to for years. One she went walking with, met for coffee, spent hours on the phone with, sharing many personal life experiences.

The two, once like sisters, had a disagreement about politics that went shockingly off the rails. The conversation quickly escalated from politics into an argument over who was right, who was wrong, who was better or worse, who was being unfair, and who needed to back off.

As each continued to stand their ground, the conversation then turned personal and ugly. Rebecca fell silent when her friend became so enraged she began to unload one petty shot after another. Going off topic completely, eventually shouting the things she had "*always* hated about Rebecca."

She went as far as to remind her of the painful and embarrassing things told in confidence along with what a good friend *she'd* been during the times Rebecca's daughter was a "strung out mess."

Each low blow a dagger to the heart.

Their conversation ended with a threat that Rebecca had "better not be caught anywhere alone in public."

How quickly it went from opposing views to weapons drawn like enemies. Madness.

Hours later, relevant passive-aggressive quotes and posts began appearing on social media as the offended woman went from **persecutor** to positioning herself as **victim** and **hero** while running a campaign of hate against Rebecca, the friend she once loved dearly.

*(Note: in my opinion when it comes to conflict and social media, **never should the two meet!** It does no good to drag your strife out for public viewing. It's an immature, nasty, low level tactic. It's also an unfair way to try to win an argument.)*

To have someone close turn on you with such velocity is beyond mind-blowing. Ever been there?

It's hard to believe anyone should even have to worry about a disagreement turning into that. These are wives, mothers, and business women...these are adults!

Conflict can get crazy and the strongest of bonds can be broken in a moment. What could have calmly been settled that day exploded into a raging battle and because of it the two were never able to recover their friendship.

Unfortunately, it's not an uncommon occurrence. Friends turning into enemies and family becoming strangers is a mystery that most of us will never solve. Conflict is *baffling*, powerful, and often involves years and layers of built up emotion, resentment, and other issues one might be carrying.

It's worth realizing when someone takes a sharp turn toward personal and vicious versus sticking to facts and efforts leading toward understanding and resolution, there *has* to be bigger, unhandled issues going on with them.

We've all been there.

There are times in the heat of conflict when, like Rebecca, it's best to step back from the relationship and deal with the effects on your own rather than chasing someone down to make them realize how you feel, what you meant, the impact of what they said, how you're hurt...and so on.

In some situations, peace can only be made internally.

When it comes to conflict, the best issues to resolve are my own.

Concerning others not treating us fair or kind, that's on them to work out. Once we have received a signal that a conflict is going to turn into viciousness or feuding, it's *our* responsibility to protect ourselves (and act right).

Whether that means to stand up for your point, defend yourself with dignity, or withdraw from the situation.

We instinctively know when we have reached a point of no return and the issues aren't going to be settled, at least not in that moment. Past that point nothing good comes about—we're only adding damage.

If the person opposing us doesn't seem to have the will or capacity to acknowledge their side of the issue without becoming venomous and upset, that's not our problem to work through.

For situations that tend to go from disagreement to combat in .03 seconds, only you are in control of how you respond and what you'll allow.

HOW DO WE HANDLE HEATED CONFLICT?

It pays to look deep within. Becoming self-aware and checking our motives is key. We can always come back to our motives.

Questions to ask ourselves:

Am I motivated for peace and solution? Or am I driving to win, making sure the other person loses? Do you have to be the bad guy for me to be good? Am I motivated by revenge? Am I trying to cause someone else to feel what I'm actually feeling inside?

Is it possible that I'm reacting out of old emotional injuries? Am I heated in *this* situation but actually my hostility is surging out of other issues going on in my life?

Is how this person's treatment of me a pattern that I need to remove from my life?

Think about it. Self-realization very often leads to solution.

At some point we have to decide we are either going to be motivated for peace or we're not. Examining your own motives and patterns will always reveal these truths. Our heart knows the honest answers to these questions if we'll get quiet and ask.

* * *

Is it worth it? We're not here on this earth forever; we don't know when a conversation with someone will be the last. Do I really want my last conversation with someone to be how *right* I was and how apologetic they needed to be? I absolutely don't.

But it's about balance. In repeat patterns of conflict, I also know that I *can't* be the one who always apologizes, who always makes peace just to keep the peace. *I can't **always** be wrong!*

There are times when someone *needs* their feet held to the fire. Others need to be accountable for behavior that is not okay for us. It's not good for anyone if we are regularly tolerating what we don't feel good about in order not to make someone uncomfortable because they can't handle being called on their stuff.

That's codependency and dysfunction.

There is a time to keep peace, there's a time to bite our tongue. There is also a time to firmly stand your ground in order for another adult to realize maybe they need to do some self-examining.

* * *

CONFLICT BOTTOM-LINES

Professional advice I was given in the years we dealt with the worst of family conflict:

You are not required to receive insults, abuse, or **vitriol**. Nor are *you* healthy when using those kinds of tactics.

Think around corners, beyond the moment I'm in. Is there a possible solution or is this just exhausting drama that will not end? Does this take my focus, energy and time away from important things such as other friends, family, priorities, and goals? Am I going to be able to undo the damage of how I'm handling this person *right now* should my feelings change or our paths cross again? Or will my words and actions in the heat of the moment make it awkward running into each other?

Interrupt the pattern when I recognize I'm in one: Stop, breathe, and modify usual responses to take a healthier direction. Regardless of discomfort. *Being healthy and functional is sometimes going to be uncomfortable!*

Do not post about it! When it comes to conflict and social media, again: never should the two meet! It's not stable to drag your strife out for public viewing. It's an immature, nasty, low-level tactic.

Settle matters in person or move on.

Leave room for amends. Always leave a space for someone (including yourself) to come to their senses and own how they acted. Don't allow yourself to go too far in once it becomes heated. It could be that they (or you) have bigger issues going on behind the scenes causing more emotion and less control.

Most important...

Take care of yourself, protect yourself, tend to yourself, be aware of yourself. We are in control of our responses and we are to be our own advocates.

And remember, *"Conflict cannot survive without your participation."* ~Wayne Dyer, from *Everyday Wisdom*, ©2005, Hay House, Inc., Carlsbad, CA

When it comes to conflict we aren't the victim, persecutor or hero; we're either participants or we're in pursuit of peace.

Chapter 23

Summer Camp, Empty Nest, and SUD: The Practice of Letting Go

"All of a sudden the nest is empty. The birds have gone, and what had been a constant blur of activity is now nothing more than a few discarded feathers. Silence mutes all that was colorful and it is time to reestablish our significant place in an ever changing world." ~ Marci Seither

All parents know the day will come when the kids will leave home and go off into life. It can be a strange, sinking time for any mom and dad. But when the launch happens abruptly and includes upsetting circumstances, it adds an extra amount of worry to the loneliness and longing you may feel over years gone by.

Huge, abrupt change is a process to work through, one day at a time. Sometimes one breath at a time. There are days you move through it moment by moment.

I myself was not prepared for the hole in my life once my son no longer lived with me. It was so engulfing at times that I felt the sadness would never lift. I had a difficult time seeing a baseball field, being around athletes, hearing things like cleats on pavement or kids laughing and playing. I felt sad, strange, and empty in those moments. Walking through a grocery store and hearing someone yell "Mom!" can send a shock wave through a mother with a child gone from them, filling our eyes with hot, unexpected tears.

I know lots of parents who have had a son or daughter

leave the home to go off to college, get married, or head off into a life of recovery after the tornado of a chemical addiction has ripped through their lives. Believe it or not, that is becoming just as common.

Whatever prompts the changes, for a while we are left with a gaping hole of emptiness and a noticeably barren schedule.

Empty nest happens, and really, it's supposed to. When it happens out of change that involved turmoil, it's not the normal "next steps of life." Even so, it can lead to good things and open up a great next phase of life for a family.

Knowing that the emptiness does pass and life can become joyful and exciting again (if we work with it) helps move us toward hope filled days again.

* * *

"To raise a child who is comfortable enough to leave you, means you've done your job. They are not ours to keep, but to teach to soar on their own." ~Unknown

When my son was little, we went to a summer camp together every year. I volunteered as an adult leader so he would have the presence of a parent with him. It was something we looked forward to every summer.

One summer, feeling confident and independent at around age 11 or 12 (and knowing many of the regular campers), he asked if he could go to camp by himself.

Meaning...without...*me.* In this moment, I realized my son was growing up.

My heart initially felt the sting of rejection. Then my mind seemed to shift gears into my usual fear-based thought patterns. Worries of all that could go wrong and that it would take over an hour for me to get to him if he needed me swirled through my mind.

Swallowing the negative thoughts, I told him I *supposed* he was old enough and probably ready, like the majority of his fellow campers, to go without his mom. So I gave him my permission. He was more thrilled than I would have liked.

Once plans were made for my absence from camp, day after day I walked around feeling heavy-hearted and sullen. Somberly going to work, brooding and mourning, silently dreading the day I would drive my son to camp and leave him there; *alone.*

Obviously I believed he could *only* survive in my care!

At that time, I worked for a man who counseled families. One afternoon, my boss asked why lately I seemed so moody and discouraged. I explained my worrisome circumstances.

Always kind yet wise, his response was;

"Oh no, don't do that. Don't impede him with your emotions—you'll hinder him. Don't put that on him. Your son is confident and independent. Isn't that what you've told me is your goal for him? Don't be the type who hangs your emotional weight on your child. Mourning over missing him is not proof that you have a great relationship! That's about you. It's selfish really. He knows you are going to miss him; he knows you love him. But if you unload the weight of this sad, pitiful display on his shoulders, making sure he knows Mom is going to cry her eyes out while he's gone, and then expect him to walk into that camp carrying your issues and enjoy himself, go swimming, fishing, do campy things and have fun while weighed down by that, you are doing him a grave disservice. Let him experience this without all that.

Tell him you'll miss him but you can't wait to hear all about it afterwards! He knows how to reach you if he needs to. Let him know; Mom and home will be waiting for him to get back. Tell him Mom may go do some fun things herself that week! Tell him he's brave! And then...let him go."

That advice was one wake-up call I never forgot—how right it was! All of it. I *had* been making it about me. And about fear. But mostly, about **me**.

We don't need to hang our sadness, worries, or issues on our sons and daughters. How *unfair* is that for them? Just like I intentionally never put on a long face when my son went for weekends with his dad (even though I spent many of them crying over his absence), how could I possibly make *this* about me, sending him off to cope with my weight on his back?

Thankful for the enlightenment, I spent the next few days with my son shopping for camping supplies, recalling great memories from previous summers, and preparing him for the new ones he'd make.

I also told him over and over how proud I was of him for wanting to go off on his own like this; what courage! With that, I gave him the emotional freedom to go without my needs and worries strangling him.

He called home twice that week, once was to tell me he caught a "huge fish" and once after he got stung by a bee. He was proud of himself for having survived the pain of it and couldn't wait to show me the mark it left.

GASP!! He didn't call me *when* it happened? Instead of feeling rejected by that, I felt relieved that he was brave enough to stay and deal. My son was learning to live and survive without me. Just as he needed to. That is not a threat to the relationship, it's evidence of coping skills our children will need for the rest of their lives.

* * *

Years later, when my son moved states away to begin a new life on his own, I often thought back to that summer camp advice from my wise boss. The awareness it gave me meant that in these new rough moments, instead of calling and sounding like a blubbering, mournful "poor mom" kind of mess, I would truthfully tell him about my grief and nostalgia, my fears, and worries. And then I'd speak of my great confidence in him and how insanely proud I am of the man he has grown into.

I am thankful to know that I don't need to make anyone responsible for how I feel. It's not the burden of our sons and daughters to bear when we feel lonely or get swept up in nostalgia. It's up to us as their parents to regulate those emotions and keep them in check. Our kids have their own life to focus on and a big world to explore.

My son knows I miss him and he knows he's loved. He is strong enough to face life with the knowledge of my love for him as a launch pad, not a liability.

The best thing we can do for our kids is to be as strong, healthy, and well as possible.

I believe much of life is about letting go. My son and I enjoy the time we have together; to the *very fullest!* Even still, my job is to encourage his strength and independence. Which allows him to build momentum on his own as an adult. And that ensures he can cope without me.

Our paths are intertwined forever. They separate, wind back around, and return adjacent to one another. That's the ebb and flow of life. Our relationship isn't threatened by that. As different as our lives are now, they're wonderful and full. We have days filled with ups and downs, joy and sorrow. There are great and terrible moments as well as lots of routine and mundane. We share our lives as often as we speak, but we are not dependent upon one another. What comfort and freedom that gives our relationship.

* * *

There are many wonderful tools and resources available that help ease the transition of empty nest, life change, and grief. Tools that help us rebuild so that life is not only manageable but joyful.

I found personal strength on the toughest of days in therapy, recovery work, a few trustworthy friends, relevant books, and the discovery of new projects to fill up the empty moments.

It's a new life for sure. But the old one was due to fade anyway.

It takes time—it's a process. It's okay to be gentle with yourself.

"Nothing is permanent, make peace with this." ~Unknown

Chapter 24

Looking Back and Moving On:
A Conversation with My Son and Elliot's Perspective on Addiction

On a recent visit home after quite some time apart, my son "Elliot" and I did a dual interview to discuss our experience roughly five years ago with substance use disorder.

Together we sat down for a very real, open conversation.

Elliot gave his perspective as one who has been to the depths of darkness with this disorder and I gave mine as a mother deeply affected. We touched some on our background and story and then went right into the most intense dynamics we faced as a family.

Relapse occurs mentally long before it occurs physically.

When asked if he ever "hit bottom," Elliot's response was, "Yes, *several* times and each time was worse than before. But life would then eventually come together again. Things would level out and almost as if forgetting, I would drift back to old mindsets again and find myself on track to another bottom." Elliot explained that it wasn't until he *decided* to live a life with different goals and began refocusing his thoughts toward staying on track that he began taking preventative steps to avoid circling back through and repeating dangerous cycles.

Family relationships will recover if you allow for

time and forgiveness.

As is common when substance abuse has raged through a family, our family dynamics were a disaster for a while. Crisis tends to bring out whatever pathological bio/psycho/socio "trash" lies dormant (meaning, it causes everyone's dysfunction to rise to the surface). There were hard feelings, bad blood, and fractured communication on all sides.

Where we are today is a far cry from where we were then. Recovery is possible and I believe it works best when everyone does individual work on themselves (therapy, relevant books, soul searching, support groups etc.). With time and compassion, we both began to realize that in the midst of some terrible circumstances, everyone was doing the best they thought they could do.

It's not personal

Regarding stressful conflict, texts that get hateful, conversations that turn toxic, and behaviors that involve betrayal, lying, stealing etc., Elliot's explanation related to a speaker he heard. The idea is that there are times we internally *commit* to choices. Sometimes we will commit to a choice even if it's the wrong one and drive it all the way home, believing it is the best choice, the *only* choice, in that moment.

When it comes to a loved one committing to a wrong choice that is having terrible effects on others, Elliot's suggestion was to not engage it, protect yourself, and back away.

When someone is deep in struggle with a dependency upon a substance, their thoughts are only on what they need to do to meet that need. Anyone they affect or argue with is either a steppingstone, a source, or in the way.

And that is exactly what the disease of addiction does. The mentality of your loved one is not only unlike the person you know and love—it's not intentional. But it is adversarial. SUD takes over the mind and will of the person struggling.

Silence is excruciating

When communication is cut off between the one struggling and the family at home, those can be extremely frightening, painful times for a parent.

I asked my son to think of what he feels if his dog is out of sight, even for a few minutes, and doesn't respond when he calls for him.

Or...what happens when he can't find his cell phone?

Those situations prompt frantic moments of panic and wild searching. Now, multiply those feelings by a million to understand what a parent goes through when their child is lost, off in active addiction, or perhaps has gone silent for days on end.

It is these emotions that drive our decisions to investigate, hunt down our sons, daughters, or other loved ones, walk the floors, and "lose it" emotionally. These were the times that I had to absolutely prop myself up on my faith because I could not control my fearful emotions.

SUD is a crisis no family should have to become great at handling.

There are ways to go about it with sound, healthy judgment. But there is no way to become perfect at handling the crisis of addiction. The reality is, it's a terrible disease that creates terrible circumstances, chaos, and emotions for anyone touched by it.

Don't go crazy in the madness of it! That will solve nothing.

During the worst of times I literally became a detective and a forensics expert. Researching, spying, tracking people, and chasing away anyone he was involved with. I even kept binoculars in my car!

Elliot made it clear this resulted in a huge breakdown in communication, furthering the breach of trust between us. It also caused him to go to greater lengths to find sources, involving much more risk and danger than usual.

Chasing him down, doing the crazy things, going mad in the midst of it helped no one, solved nothing, and didn't cause anyone or anything to get better.

Had I put up healthy boundaries, enforced consequences, while maintaining a kinder, more logical position, and then taken my hands off, we may have been better able to discuss solutions sooner than we did. Looking back, I did the best I could with the tools I had. We all did. But if I had it to do again, I would have taken a softer approach and been fully equipped with the CRAFT method in place.

It took time for us *both* to heal from those days.

There's hope

Elliot's advice to those who are in their teens, 20s, and 30s who may wrestle with a dependency or SUD (regardless of how it began), is that it life doesn't have to be about leaning on a substance or who can party the hardest. "At the end of the day you end up sloppy and might find yourself living down current choices for decades to come."

Elliot's words for anyone caught in the trap of active use who feels lost, alone, hopeless, or like there is no way out: "Please know there are thousands of hands out there ready to help you. You can find a meeting (NA, AA etc.) taking place every day in your city. All you have to do is call, show up, reach out."

His hope for families was to let them know when he came to the end of every resource and had to become his *own* solution, he then had to find his way. That is what drove him to the desire for sobriety, recovery, and a healthy productive life.

We are all relieved with how far he's come (and how far we've come as a family) these last four years.

Recovery works on many levels.

I later asked my son when he was back home for a visit if it bothered him to go into old, familiar places or potentially cross paths with people he may have hard feelings toward (or vice versa). I wondered because those things tend to bother me.

His response was, "Not at all. Places don't affect me anymore like they used to. As for people, I'm aware of energy and vibes. If someone is negative and rude, it just tells me that the person hasn't dealt with their own unresolved issues. That's all. I've moved on."

Once you heal and move forward, you really can be done with the residual effects.

We are aware of the work of recovery and its power in our lives in how completely our relationship has healed. A wonderful aspect of having gone through the nightmare of addiction in the family is that due to the level crisis we reached, we were forced to learn how to deal with deep issues. We now know great ways to face and manage struggles and then put them behind us. There's no elephant in the room today, no junk swept under the rug that we have to ignore when we sit down to dinner, or have a visit. We live in the wholeness of the moment and celebrate life as it is right *now*. Looking back only to learn and reminisce, but focusing forward on where we are and what lies ahead.

"The future belongs to those who believe in the beauty of their dreams." ~ Eleanor Roosevelt

Never give up!

Chapter 25

I'm No Victim

What does it even mean to be a victim? To settle this for myself, I found a three-part definition.

Victim: *a person harmed or injured; a person tricked or duped; a person who suffers injury or destruction.*

Victim: *A person harmed or injured*

When one becomes harmed or injured, we first grapple with the affects. The validity of what has occurred shouldn't be denied. For a time and depending on the type and severity, we need to melt down and allow ourselves the time to feel miserable about what has occurred.

As for wallowing? I have a rule: *At first I must! But don't gather dust.* After a time of upset or grief, we need to begin the work toward healing and recovering.

I've been harmed and injured enough to know how important it is to correctly heal. If a bone isn't set right, it will remain painful and deformed. Our soul is no different.

* * *

Victim: *A person tricked or duped*

"A company of wolves is better than a company of wolves in sheep's clothing." ~ Unknown

I think most of us have been a victim of being duped!

"Be careful who you are charmed by—instead of

thinking someone *is* charming, it's first wise to ask *why* they might be charming you?"

That was some of the best advice I've been given. Strong connections that happen quickly are now a red flag for me. As is someone declaring (or posting) how marvelous and good hearted they are. I have fallen for manufactured sincerity and false kindness more times than I could ever count (and paid dearly for it). It's not selfish to be cautious—it's healthy.

As much as being duped or tricked might have happened when dealing with a loved one in the grips of active addiction, due to *my* dysfunctional family patterns and fractured confidence, for me it occurred most often in friendships with women.

I used to open myself up completely, only to get hurt by the same types of betrayals and manipulations over and over again. I would repeatedly cry and complain about the same old scenarios but then put myself back around it. Sometimes for years.

At some point, deciding to take the reins of our lives and not play the part of someone easy to prey on leads us toward safety, wisdom and health.

* * *

Victim: *A person who suffers injury or destruction*

Interesting to me that the word *suffers* in this part of the definition is present tense.

I am acutely aware that if I allow myself, I could mentally rehearse events from before, even from a few years ago, and end up down a rabbit hole of bitterness. I choose not to because I don't want to suffer *presently* for injuries behind me.

A few weeks ago, I complained to an old friend about an insulting comment from a relative of mine on social media. Having once experienced something similar from the same person, my friend went into a heated rant about having it happen to him...when he was in the *seventh grade.*

Telling it again, he was as angry and affected as if he had just experienced it. I didn't know how to console that, other than to bring the conversation forward a few decades.

Comparably, when my son played baseball we spent a season traveling with four families from out of state. I never forgot a divorced couple in the group. Both seemed fun and friendly. However, as soon as her ex-husband was out of ear shot, the ex-wife would openly insult him and reveal embarrassing, personal things about him and members of his family. She detailed the misery of being married to him. Her insults were openly said in front of their kids.

Often ending her awkward narrative with a lament about how, being stuck with this divorce and the children she is raising alone, she will "never have a healthy relationship, her life is ruined...all because of him."

It was astonishing that she was that stuck in blame and so caught in her perceived injuries from years prior that she didn't seem to notice people were uncomfortable hearing about them. She mistook polite discomfort as interest. She was oblivious to herself. By the same token, we came to respect him for never once speaking ill of her.

We often repel others with our own poisoned spirits and sometimes we do it unaware. I believe we can become blinded by bitterness. This woman could have made the best of a disappointing situation, instead of dragging others back through it for years to come.

We may be injured and even for a time destroyed. But we don't have to *continue* suffering for the rest of our life. That part is a choice.

Pain, rejection, betrayal, loss, failure, and so on—these things come to interrupt us as we journey forward in life. We aren't supposed sit down permanently in those interruptions.

Recently, I heard a successful speaker say something I loved: *"I may have been thrown under the bus, but I kept getting up and now I'm driving it."*

She rose up from a past full of personal heartache to go on and make a huge career out of helping people better themselves. She took the wheel of her life.

* * *

I decided years ago for myself that I too would overcome and try to triumph through the hard times instead of getting stuck and being a victim of the hand I was dealt. If that meant reading self-help books until my eyeballs fell out, spending every extra dollar on therapy, meditating and praying myself to sleep, and hitting every support group in town, I was willing do it!

Wellness is everything—recovery works.

I'm personally determined not to spend my life stuck in what didn't go well. I decided I wanted to have a *life!* We have a decision to make. We can either live our lives bitter and stuck in the wreckage, or we can reclaim life, take it by the reins, and go for every ounce of the wholeness, peace, and joy available.

* * *

No blame in my game

When we catch ourselves growing bitter and negative, it pays to stop and ask, "Who am I blaming my life

163

on?" The truth is, we are responsible for our own lives. Taking charge of that separates us from the internal bonfire of resentment that is always ready to rise up if we have someone to point a finger at for how we've failed or been let down.

See ya later Self-pity

Self-pity is defined as *"The self-indulgent belief that my life is harder and sadder than anyone else's."*

Taking the pulse of how sorry we feel for ourselves reminds us to focus inward and to look forward. We have much to be thankful for if we stop to realize it and much more life to be lived ahead. It's up to us to go after it.

We can choose fluid forgiveness versus forced remorse

When possible, I don't make an issue of getting an apology. If I was still waiting on an apology for every slight and disappointment in my life, I'd be the unhappiest person imaginable.

You can't spend your life depending on someone else's remorse in order to let go and get over it. When it comes to that, think of life as a stream. It's healthiest to keep the current clear of debris, let go of it and keep on flowing forward.

You're no one's doormat and you are no one's dartboard. But if you do get stomped on, or have darts thrown at you, it will hurt. It might even drop you. But you can recover, rise, and keep running this race. If you decide to.

* * *

Working the damages through, recovery IS possible

When my son started reading my first book, he called to tell me he hadn't known a few things from my childhood. Like for instance, how I lost the hearing in my right ear. Nor did he know many of the profoundly difficult circumstances of family dysfunction and poverty through my early school years.

We talked a bit about some of that, even laughing about some of the craziness we've lived through. I asked him in reference to one particular difficulty I experienced as a child, "And can *you* believe no one even told me I was going to kindergarten?? They just sent me in with no explanation!" He responded "No really I can't. But...you're okay."

I **loved** that response. Because yeah, I am. I'm okay. I'm no victim.

I don't deny and avoid hurt or harm in my life by any means. I choose to face it, feel it, work it through, and flourish.

I love that my son didn't seem to grow up marinating in my misery. In fact he wasn't even aware of most of it! My hope is that my life as well as my personality show no real evidence of past heartache and injury unless I decide to tell it with grace and dignity. It's possible—when we choose to recover.

Recovery, it works if you work it and we are all worth it.

Life is what we make it!

Never give up!

Afterword

Though our story as of yet has no ending, this chapter of life is closing so new ones may begin.

"Unbroken" came to be in the "midnight hour" of our story. When despair, loneliness and the condition of my life drove me to write around the clock in order to: 1. Heal myself forward and 2. Release the poison I felt full of.

I promised my father when he was in hospice 15 years prior I would always fight to keep a triumphant mind regardless of my circumstances. That no matter how low life dropped me, I would always set my mind to *get back UP*. He advised me to latch myself onto a goal in the midst of bad times as a way to rise from them with strength and dignity. That was his reassurance that sending me into my 30's fatherless didn't mean I would be weak, uncared for, or easy prey when facing life's hardships.

The promise has not always been easy to keep. At times I wanted to slouch from the wall to the floor and sit forever in a puddle of "Poor me, how can this possibly be my life?" lamentations. But a promise like that doesn't just evaporate from your memory. It rises within when you need it the most.

So here I found myself, a decade and a half later, remembering the stoic commitment I swore myself to as I faced some of the greatest moments of pain, fear, humiliation, hopelessness, and isolation of my life. In the midst of what felt like the worst, I applied the promise. For every setback, I set a goal. For every piece of news that dropped me to my knees, I wrote for hours, offering comfort to someone else. For every kick in the teeth from someone close to me, I walked miles thanking the Source of my strength in alphabetical order for something I was blessed with or would eventually accomplish: **A**mazing strength, **B**ig plans for the future, **C**ompassion and **C**omfort... **M**ountains that are moving...**P**eace and **P**rotection...a **S**uccess **S**tory of redemption...**T**riumph despite how much I've lost...**U**nshakeable faith...**V**ictory over it all. And on and on, from A to Z. I would pour it out, sometimes a dozen times a day.

Day after day, month after month, I fought back for my life with relentless effort and stubborn hope despite little proof that *any* of it would matter.

As winter gave way to spring, slowly life began to thaw and turn in my favor. I give credit to keeping that promise to my father. Keeping it meant I didn't get to feel sorry for myself or hinge the blame for my life on anyone else. It kept me fighting on, getting back up, trying again, looking beyond myself, and finding my way forward despite my circumstances.

The pages of this book are filled with the sorrows of my heart as much as they illustrate a certain *something* resident deep down within. That "something" we all have. It can't be seen, explained, or understood. Neither can it be extinguished. It's a fighting spirit. One that ignites if we allow it. Fanned into flames, it lifts us and launches us upward, onward, forward, before hope even seems possible.

And somehow as we go, that hope starts to grow stronger. And then just like the dawn, breakthroughs appear.

In the misery of your own midnight hour, may you as

well make a promise to yourself and in honor of those you had to let go of too soon; to somehow, *someway* find it possible to rise from the ashes no matter how impossibly dark and finished your life might seem to be. And slowly, eventually, yet *powerfully,* you too will rise—Unbroken.

NOTHING is impossible. Never give up!

Annie Highwater is a Writer, Speaker, Podcast Host and Family Advocate. She is a life-long researcher of Behavioral Science with particular interests in family pathology and concepts of dysfunction, addiction, alcoholism and conflict. In 2016, Annie published her memoir, *Unhooked: A Mother's Story of Unhitching from the Roller Coaster of Her Son's Addiction.* Her story is especially relevant in helping us all understand the personal challenges facing the affected parents and family members, and how family dynamics both help and hinder the recovery process. Annie resides in Columbus, Ohio and enjoys writing, long distance running, hiking, the great outdoors and visiting her son in Southern California as often as possible.

Mission Statement:

There are more people affected by addiction than there are people addicted. My mission is to promote healthy dialogue and to offer support, information and hope to the stressed out, affected family, partners and friends (basically the "entourage") of those in the grips of addiction, alcoholism and SUD.

www.anniehighwater.com

www.twitter.com/mindyanne1991

www.facebook.com/AnnieUnhooked

9 781939 844521